THE TRADITION OF
WESTERN MUSIC

THE

TRADITION

OF

WESTERN MUSIC

GERALD ABRAHAM

UNIVERSITY OF CALIFORNIA PRESS

BERKELEY   LOS   ANGELES

University of California Press
Berkeley and Los Angeles, California

Copyright © 1974, by
Gerald Abraham

ISBN: 0-520-02414-1

Library of Congress Catalog Card Number: 72-97738

Printed in Great Britain

CONTENTS

The Ernest Bloch Professorship of Music and the Ernest Bloch Lectures were established at the University of Calfornia in 1962 in order to bring distinguished figures in music to the Berkeley campus from time to time. Made possible by the Jacob and Rosa Stern Musical Fund, the professorship was founded in memory of Ernest Bloch (1880-1959), Professor of Music at Berkeley from 1940 to 1959.

THE ERNEST BLOCH PROFESSOR

1964	RALPH KIRKPATRICK
1965-66	WINTON DEAN
1966-67	ROGER SESSIONS
1968-69	GERALD ABRAHAM
1971	LEONARD B. MEYER
1972	EDWARD T. CONE

AUTHOR'S NOTE

The ideas underlying these lectures, given at the University of California (Berkeley) in April and May 1969, developed from a paper on 'Creating a Musical Tradition' read to the Royal Society of Arts, London, on 25 January 1967. In preparing the lectures for the press I have expanded one or two passages, revised some others, and added footnote references and further musical examples, but I have made no attempt to disguise their origin in the spoken word. I warmly thank my friends Daniel Heartz and Helen Farnsworth for respectively reading over my manuscript and retyping it.

THE NATURE OF MUSICAL TRADITION

Why 'tradition'? And why 'Western music'? Tradition of every kind is much spat upon nowadays and to label anything 'Western' is to sound overtones of racialism and politics, or at best to suggest a deplorably limited outlook. The very word 'tradition' conveys to many people the idea of something static, mummified; I do not know who first spoke of 'the dead hand of tradition', but his conception of tradition is regrettably widespread. Unthinking lip-service to tradition or being overawed by a sense of tradition can have dreadful consequences in music as in anything else; as Mahler said of the way things were done at the Vienna Opera, 'Tradition is slovenliness.' But this is tradition misconceived. The true essence of tradition, as I see it and propose to discuss it, is perpetual life and change, very often slow and organic, yet often modified—sometimes quite violently modified—by external circumstances. And I have chosen to limit my subject to 'Western music', by which I mean the music of Europe and America, not because I suppose it to be more valuable than other kinds of music but because I know more about it than about other kinds; because in many respects it is fundamentally different from other musics; above all because it offers by far the best field for study of a living musical tradition or traditions over a long period. Other musical high-cultures, the Indian and the Chinese, for instance, are as old as ours or older, but we lack the means to study their life-history and they seem to us, perhaps wrongly, to have developed at very leisurely tempi. The tempo of Western musical evolution was like that during the first Christian millennium but has gradually been getting faster, right down to the bewildering pace of today.

The long tradition of Western music also fascinates by its complexity, a complexity which I must try to elucidate by probing it with questions of 'how' and 'why'. It is not simply a matter of forms or techniques or ways and conditions of performing music. There emerges something much more subtle, an underlying ethos which is hardly definable but which we Westerners feel and comprehend instinctively because we are a part of it, whereas the ethos of another music, Indian, Chinese, or whatever, necessarily eludes us even though we may carefully and lovingly study its form and techniques.

The working of a living musical tradition can be studied in its simplest form in the handing down of a folk-song. Cecil Sharp in his classic book on English folk-song illustrated it in this way:[1]

> Let us suppose that an individual, A, invents a story and tells it to his friend, B. B, if the story takes hold of him, will narrate it to C, but in doing so will consciously or unconsciously—it matters not which—make some changes in the tale. He will very likely locate it in his own neighbourhood, change the names of the *dramatis personae* to those of his own friends and relatives, and in countless small ways 'improve' upon the tale as he received it from A. C, in passing on the story to D, will, in like manner, add to it his own 'improvements'. D, E, F, etc. will follow the same example. . . . By the time it reaches Z we may . . . conceive that the story has become so changed that it bears no longer any resemblance to the form in which it originally left the mouth of A. . . . For simplicity's sake we have assumed that A related his story to one friend only. But in all probability he would tell it to many others as well. Instead, therefore, of one B, there will be many B's. Now each of the latter will in turn relate the story . . . to his own circle of friends . . . [and] the number of those concerned in the transmission of the story will increase at every step . . . by geometrical progression.

This process of transmission has bedevilled one form of tradition with which many of us are concerned: traditions of performance, of interpretation. Faced with some problem of *musica ficta* or ornamentation or *continuo* realization, we may wish that tradition would show us its 'dead hand' a little more often than it does. (The 'dead

[1] *English Folk-Song: Some Conclusions* (London, 1907), pp. 10-11.

hold some aces.) Of course it does sometimes, first those early German treatises on organ-playing, like *Fundamentum* of 1452, which record for us practical examples of interpretation. From that time onward we have three centuries of such records: how to ornament Palestrina's vocal lines, how to 'grace' Purcell's or Handel's, how Corelli himself is said to have played those violin *adagios* that look so simple on paper. And with the advent of the *basso continuo* we have similar records suggesting how the bass line might be filled out by the keyboard-player, though all too seldom telling how some notable composer actually did it. Yet, however valuable these are to us in our endeavour to recapture the authentic ways of performing old music, they give us only glimpses of the real process that went on all the time. We cannot trace the traditions of performance that were handed down from master to pupil or copied from the practice of great artists, and so constituted a continuum in which every musician —at any rate in a given area—participated and to which he contributed, no matter how humbly or even unfortunately. These were traditions of musical sense and feeling, a great unbroken historical procession which we see only in a rough sketch made at one point, a more finished picture made at another—no more.

Mechanical means have changed all that, though the earliest mechanical means, the metronome, which recorded only the composer's own tempi, was not too happy a beginning. Beethoven's probably inaccurate and Schumann's certainly inaccurate metronomes have left us as many problems as they solved. But thanks to the phonograph we know exactly how Grieg played his *An die Frühling* (like a sentimental schoolgirl) and how Stravinsky conducted *Petrushka*. The irony of the coming of the phonograph is that it happened too late: too late to record the interpretations of the period when interpretation was more vital than at any time before or since, the period when music became primarily a message, the romantic period. To take ornamentation alone: the treatises of the baroque period tell us what notes to play, but with Chopin or Liszt that is generally clear enough and in any case what matters is not *what* but *how*, with what subtle nuances of tone and shading, rhythm

3

and dynamics. And we have nothing to tell us except inadequate notation and hearsay: tradition. We know how Chopin played only through the playing of the pupils of the pupils of his pupils. This is the process of Cecil Sharp's story-teller; I doubt whether the traditions of how Chopin or even Clara Schumann played are much more reliable.

In the transmission of folk-song we get no such glimpses of tradition in action as we do in the transmission of performing practice—or very few. But we can be confident about the nature of the process, which was dynamic in the way that live musical tradition always is. I need hardly say that I am using the term 'folk-song' in its precise meaning, not in one of the various senses in which the word is loosely applied nowadays but as it is defined by Cecil Sharp and formulated by Maud Karpeles,[2] the product of three elements: continuity, variation, and selection:

> Continuity, which preserves the tradition; variation, which springs from individual creative impulse; selection, which pronounces the verdict of the community. A folk-song is anonymous not merely because the original author has been forgotten, but because it has been fashioned and re-fashioned through many generations by countless individual singers.

A man heard a song—whether the song originated with a court musician, a poet or a peasant is immaterial—and, as it was not noted down or he was unable to read notation, he sang it from memory. He may have sung it almost correctly the first time but as he grew older and his memory grew more hazy, it would become less like the original. He would sing it more and more the way he liked it; in fact, it is well known that peasant-singers will change a song almost from day to day; and the way he liked it may or may not have been an improvement on the original. Others would hear him and sing the song in their ways, even confusing it with the words and tunes of other songs. So the process continued until the folk-song collector came along with his notebook or phonograph or tape-recorder and halted it. For directly a folk-song has been fixed

[2] *Grove's Dictionary* (fifth edition), III, p. 183.

in notation it ceases to be a folk-song; it becomes simply a record of one form of a folk-song at a moment of time. It has become a museum-piece in the best sense of the word, something we can all enjoy; but it is no longer living art, except in so far as the peasants may go on singing the song in their various ways after the collector has left the village. As it happens, in many cases—from John and Lucy Broadwood and Cecil Sharp with English and Appalachian folk-song to Frances Densmore with the American Indians—the early collectors came along only just in time to preserve for the museum a good range of specimens of what was already a dying art.

In this process by which folk-song comes into being we have a sort of parable of the formation of all musical tradition. We do not know how any folk-song began, though we can speculate sometimes, or what it was like when it began. We do not know how music itself began, though philosophers and musicologists have produced all sorts of plausible and implausible theories—including Darwin's, in *The Descent of Man*, that it all started with the mating-calls of animals. Nor do we know what it was like when it began, though again we may speculate. But we speculate rather less confidently now that those ethnomusicologists who used to call themselves 'comparative musicologists' are content to study the music of primitive cultures for its own sake without imagining that the musical practices of the most backward peoples in the twentieth century necessarily throw light on the musical practices of our own palaeolithic ancestors. To believe that, one must believe that culture always progresses (in the sense of becoming more sophisticated), never regresses: a proposition that can be refuted by dozens of examples from cultural history. The music of a primitive culture may be the last decadent remnant if not of a high culture, at any rate of a less low one. The last states of a folk-song may be artistically inferior to its original form.

The evolution of a folk-song pre-figures the evolution of musical tradition in other respects than the impenetrable darkness that surrounds its origin. The 'individual creative impulse' which Dr. Karpeles specifies as one of the three essentials in the transmission of folk-song, and which (innumerably multiplied) becomes the

5

contribution of 'the folk' to the process, consists partly of a negatively selective process (the singer's memory rejecting details of the song he did not particularly like), partly of a positive one (singing the song the way *he* liked it). And there is the reciprocal essential, 'the verdict of the community' which in the same way forgot Tom's version because it didn't care for it particularly, but remembered the versions of Dick and Harry and went on singing and altering them because it *liked* those versions best. (I must repeat: the surviving versions of a folk-song are not necessarily what *we* might consider 'the best' or 'the most beautiful'; they are the ones that appealed most to the people who sang them and listened to them.) A great number of versions of some favourite songs have come down to us, but they must be only a small proportion of those lost by the way. In the nature of the thing, we know only the end-forms and can get a glimpse of some intermediary stage only from chance preservation in a more sophisticated composition. (Unfortunately, from this point of view, composers in the past preferred to borrow new popular tunes rather than old favourites: the so-called 'folk-songs' in Elizabethan virginal music were popular songs of the day; they had not begun to be folk-songs in the scientific sense.) But if we could get hold of the case-history of a folk-song in all the stages of its evolution, as we (almost) can with a Beethoven theme in his sketch-books, we should want to ask a lot of fascinating questions: Why did this or that singer prefer it that way? Why did others come to prefer his version and forget about others? We should be able to hazard only very tentative answers, even if we could ask the questions.

* * *

Fortunately this is not the case if we ask the same questions of a general musical tradition, the tradition of a particular country, for instance. Its composers, great and small, good and bad, work in that tradition and enrich it or debase it or leave it pretty much where it was. Since we know their work or can know it, and generally know something about how their public responded to it, we can ask these questions 'how' and 'why', and go on with some confidence to answer them. In fact we must answer them if we want to write a genuine history of a country's music and not a mere chronicle of events and composers' names and works. For a country's musical history does not consist of music alone; it consists also of reaction to music—or non-reaction. It would be straining a paradox to contend that Berlioz has no place in the French musical tradition; he was actually the end-product of a side-development of which we are almost totally oblivious, the French Gluckists of the Revolutionary period, the so-called 'Conservatoire composers'; but, considering the greatness of his genius, he has been *allowed to contribute* (I put it that way advisedly) astonishingly little to the tradition of French music. The importance of Bach in the German musical tradition was apparent not in his lifetime but in the successive waves of quite different influences which followed in the nineteenth and early twentieth centuries: the Bach who fascinated the real romantics, Mendelssohn and Schumann, for instance, was paradoxically very different from the 'romantic Bach' preached by Albert Schweitzer. It is fairly easy to explain why Bach made relatively little impact on the Germany of his own day, but it is noteworthy that at least a subsidiary reason was a non-musical one. His music was behind the times, that was one reason, but the state of music-publishing in the first half of the eighteenth century, as compared with what it was in the nineteenth, was another. And one can explain the Bach vogue of the earlier nineteenth century as 'historicism', and the 'romantic Bach' as the result of Pirro's and Schweitzer's exciting misconception of the nature of baroque musical symbolism. But the failure of Berlioz to leave any significant mark on the course of French music is more puzzling, though I shall try to offer an explanation later.

The closest approximation we can make to this phenomenon of the creative working of musical tradition on the smallest scale, comparable with folk-song yet firmly documented, is the evolution of certain German chorale-melodies in the couple of centuries between Luther and Bach. In some cases we can trace this from before Luther, for the melodies sometimes originated in plainsong. Plainsong itself had its period, a very long period, of purely oral transmission: in the case of the oldest melodies, several centuries

7

before they were even sketchily recorded in the imperfect mnemonic notation of unheighted neumes, and several more before a means of precisely indicating relative pitch was discovered—at which point it becomes apparent that some German monasteries had fallen into the habit of singing wider intervals than the French did.[3] Where the primitive neumes indicated an indeterminate rise and fall, the later scribes of these monasteries sometimes notated a rise or fall of perhaps a third instead of a tone—an early instance of the way in which national characteristics in music begin to establish themselves. And I need hardly remind you of the efforts of Charlemagne to establish uniformity in liturgical music throughout his empire for political reasons—an early instance of political interference in musical tradition.

The melody whose adventures I want to follow in some detail belongs to a much later period. The words of the Advent hymn 'Veni, redemptor gentium' go back to the fourth century but the melody seems to be no older than the early twelfth. All the same, it has come down to us in several minor variant forms: for instance, the word 'ostende' is sung in one version to three repeated notes, in another to three notes ascending scalewise. But it was a much loved melody, particularly in Germany; it is significant that the two oldest manuscripts in which it is found are both German, and four centuries later the German Protestants lost no time in providing it with German words. The Protestant extremist Thomas Müntzer published in 1524 a translation which begins:

> O Herr, Erlöser alles Volks,
> komm, zeig uns die Geburt deins Sohns,
> es wundern sich all Creaturen
> dass Christ also ist Mensch worden.

In 1531 it appeared in one of the German song-books of the Bohemian Brethren, Michael Weisse's *Ein New Gesengbuchlen*, with a completely new text. Both these German texts were fitted to the plainsong with only minimal changes in the actual notes, though

---

[3] Peter Wagner, *Einführung in die gregorianischen Melodien*, II (*Neumenkunde*), (Leipzig, 1912), pp. 443–7.

8

even the fitting of different vowels and consonants to plainsong produces a certain change of character. Here are (*a*) the plainsong in probably its earliest surviving form,[4] (*b*) the version with Müntzer's words:

Ex. 1 *(a)*

Luther went farther than this. In the same year as Müntzer, 1524, he printed in his so-called *Achtliederbuch* not only the translation which is sung to this day, 'Nun komm der Heiden Heiland', but a metrical modification of the melody which removes it from the sphere of plainsong to that of German song. This version was not meant to be sung by a monastic choir, as the plainsong was, nor by a little sectarian body such as a congregation of Bohemian Brethren. We know fairly well how the early Lutheran hymns were sung: not harmonized or by a trained choir or supported by an organ, but by the whole congregation in unison led by a choir of schoolboys who had had the hymns drilled into them by rote. The boys were sometimes scattered among the adult congregation; sometimes the cantor himself stood in the middle of the church. In these conditions the flexibility of plainsong was impossible; something firm, steady and

---

[4] From Maria-Einsiedeln, Stiftsbibl. 366. Printed by Bruno Stäblein, *Monumenta Monodica Medii Aevi*, I (Kassel and Basel, 1956), p. 273.

square-cut like German secular song of the time was needed. (Why German secular song tended to be square-cut is a matter that will have to be dealt with later.) The first note of a hymn-tune is often written as a long one, presumably to give the congregation a moment to pick up the pitch sounded by the cantor and his boys; the phrases are separated by pauses. But Luther's substitution of firmly stressed, rhyming heptasyllables for the smooth octosyllabic Latin verse necessitated changes in the melody itself. The plainsong has only one interval greater than a third (and that is smoothed out in the second oldest manuscript). By the removal of an intermediate note near the very beginning of the tune, Luther at once gives it a bolder outline with a leap of a fourth. In the second phrase, for the two equal notes to 'partum' he substitutes a longer and a shorter: a dotted quarter-note and an eighth-note to match the differently weighted syllables of '-frauen'. And instead of the floating movement with which the melodic curve reaches its apex on 'virginis', where it seems to hang in the air for half a breath, he brings it down with firm masculinity on 'er*kannt.*' Here and there pairs of notes in the original line suggest to him pairs of quasi-ornamental eighth-notes. And most characteristic of all the changes, for his last line, 'Gott solch Geburt ihm bestellt,' Luther totally discards the plainsong phrase and substitutes a repetition of the first phrase of the melody, rounding off and firmly tying up the four-line stanza:

Ex. 2

Nun komm der Hei - den Hei - land, der Jung-frau - en Kind er - kannt.

dass sich wun-dert al - le Welt, Gott solch Ge-burt ihm— be-stellt.

Although Luther created in 'Nun komm der Heiden Heiland' a classic conjunction of verse and music which has endured with few changes right through Bach's time and our own day, he had not yet finished with the plainsong melody. Valentin Babst's volume of

Geystliche Lieder, published in 1545, contains two other sets of words by Luther adapted to other modifications of the 'Veni, redemptor' melody, and I want to trace the adventures of one of these. It begins:

> Verleih uns Frieden gnädiglich,
> Herr Gott, zu unsern Zeiten.
> Es ist ja doch kein ander nicht,
> der für uns könnte streiten,
> denn du, unser Gott alleine.

Here we have a five-line stanza of alternating octosyllables and heptasyllables in place of the four lines of heptasyllables in 'Nun, komm'.

As later Lutheran song-books seldom fail to point out, this is the age-old prayer 'Da pacem, Domine' 'geteutscht' within a framework of metre and rhyme. Why, therefore, did Luther not mate his translation with a modification of the plainsong 'Da pacem'? And why did his choice fall instead on 'Veni, redemptor'? I think the answer is fairly clear. The opening phrase of 'Da pacem':

Ex. 3

is very like that of 'Veni, redemptor'. This near-identity of phrases is not surprising. It is not merely that the composer of plainsong usually had no more than eight or so notes at his disposal and often used only six; originality was much less important to him that it is to us. Or, rather, originality lay in different things. Plainsong composers—and the composers of old Jewish chant, the composers of Arabic music, the anonymous original composers of European folk-songs—employed conventional, traditional phrases as a baroque or classical European composer employed three- or four-note motives. Originality lay not in the units of composition but in what one did with them. After all, opening and cadential phrases can be fairly stereotyped in Western music generally, not only in plainsong.

(Even the verbal phrases and ideas of folk-song also tend to be formulae. How many English folk-songs begin with the singer walking out one May morning and meeting a fair young maid—or some such words.) So when Luther considered the plainsong 'Da pacem' he was naturally enough reminded of 'Veni, redemptor'. Whether or not he tried with no great success to adapt the 'Da pacem' music first, it is clear that the other melody was a favourite of his, so (nothing loath) he used 'Veni, redemptor' again—actually modifying it less than for the words of 'Nun komm, der Heiden Heiland'. You will notice, for instance, the cadence at 'zu unsern Zeiten' as compared with 'Kind erkannt' in the other hymn. This time he uses the fourth phrase of the plainsong, which he had rejected in 'Nun komm' in favour of a repeat of the first phrase. Even so, he had insufficient music for the last line of his poetic stanza, so he had to compose an additional phrase for 'denn du, unser Gott alleine'. Here is the result as printed in Babst's *Geystliche Lieder*:

Ex. 4

This 'Verleih uns Frieden' version of 'Veni, redemptor' had a more eventful history than the 'Nun komm' version. It would be wearisome to trace it in detail through the various Lutheran hymn-books. It will suffice to look at three or four stages of that history: the *Melodeyen-Gesangbuch* published at Hamburg in 1604, which contains an anonymous four-part setting, Hans Leo Hassler's version in his *Psalmen und geistliche Lieder ... simpliciter gesetzt* (Nuremberg, 1608), Johann Hermann Schein's in his Leipzig

Cantional of 1627, and the setting with which Bach concludes his Cantata No. 42, 'Am Abend aber,' which dates from 1725.[5] These are all simple four-part, note-against-note settings for popular use—the days of unaccompanied congregational singing were over—not forms of the tune modified for polyphonic treatment. (I quote the melodies only, and Bach's version is transposed up a semitone to facilitate comparison.) Whereas Hassler's version differs so little from Luther's that there is no need to quote it—he only elaborates the end of the last phrase—the anonymous Hamburg arranger makes some significant changes, by far the most important of which result from his application of the principles of *musica ficta*. He sharpens all the Fs, transforming the modal melody into modern G minor, and he also sharpens the C between the Ds of the third phrase—though not, of course, the passing-note C he has inserted just afterwards between D and B flat:[6]

Ex. 5

Ver - leih uns Frie - den gnä - dig - lich,   Herr Gott, zu un - sern Zei - ten.

Es   ist   doch   ja___   kein   and' - rer___   mehr,

der für uns könn - te strei - ten,   denn du un - ser Gott al - lei - ne.

Schein, more than twenty years later, does not adopt this more 'modern' version of the tune; the important difference in his version is interesting because it shows the vigorous intervention of a creative mind. Just as Luther himself took out the last phrase in 'Nun komm, der Heiden Heiland' and substituted a repeat of the first phrase to clinch the form, Schein takes out the penultimate phrase of 'Verleih

[5] Alfred Dürr, 'Zur Chronologie der Leipziger Vokalwerke J. S. Bachs', *Bach Jahrbuch*, Jg. 44 (1957), p. 130.
[6] Reprinted by Hans Albrecht, *Organum*, no. 26 (Lippstadt, 1950).

uns', the music of 'der für uns könnte streiten', and substitutes something completely different which musically 'rhymes' with the previous phrase: 'uns könnte streiten' gets the same music as 'kein ander nicht'. The intention was obviously to strengthen the inner organization of the tune:

Ex. 6

Bach's version, just a century later than Schein's, is firmly in the modern minor and, again like the anonymous Hamburg composer, he fills in the leap of a third in the third phrase with a passing note—but then, very characteristically, he fills in every potential third-leap with a passing-note. But he adopts, or rather adapts, Schein's version of the fourth phrase, although 'uns könnte streiten' is no longer a mere repetition of 'kein ander nicht':

Ex. 7

Finally let us compare that with Bach's version of 'Nun komm, der Heiden Heiland', his simple chorale treatment of it in Cantata No. 36, 'Schwingt freudig':

Ex. 8

Lob sei Gott den Va - ter g'thon,

Lob sei Gott sein'n ein' - gen Sohn, Lob sei Gott den

heil'— gen Geist im - mer und in E - wig - keit!

The two tunes still have the third phrase more or less in common, but little else except general style. Although both are descended in easily traceable steps from the same original, they are more closely related by that common style than either is to the original from which both drew their substance. Nothing could illustrate more vividly the changes that can be wrought by human attrition in a century or two—and this with music which was at each stage not only written down but published. How much more freely must the process work in the field of folk-song.

* * *

The process seen in action here is a miniature image of the working of musical tradition on the widest scale, not merely on a single melody but on whole musical styles and the ethos they reflect. However music has originated—as an instrument of magic, as a medium of emotional expression, as an artefact made for the pleasure of the artificer—it has evolved or failed to evolve within the conditions of the most various human needs and environments. The plainsong hymn was called into being very early in the history of the Church by the need of Christian communities for a form of music in which all could join in worship. For a dozen centuries, as long as Western Christianity was a unity unsplit by anything more serious than transient heresies or Papal schism, the hymn underwent local but not essential changes. The Reformation brought a whole array of new factors to bear upon it. The new faith, nurtured by the ideas of humanism, called for popularization; hymns must be understood by the people in the widest sense and performed by the people. The impact of a new language, with vowels and consonants as different as German is from Latin, to say nothing of the structure of the language and the marked stresses of German, in itself would have been considerable. But it was by no means all. Also in the interests of popularization were the approximation to the style of German secular song, the provision of a rhyming translation, and apparently a more marked separation of the phrases in congregational singing. The difference from plainsong was further widened by the four-part block harmonizations which began to be published at once (though not at first for congregational use), with a fresh chord for each melody-note and gradually more marked tonal cadences underlining the end of each phrase. Certainly the last traces of rhythmic flexibility had disappeared by Schein's day, for he follows the unbarred harmonization of 'Nun komm, der Heiden Heiland' in his *Cantional* of 1627 with a quadratically barred five-part harmonization 'in Contrapuncto'. And, of course, nothing could be more four-square than Bach's chorale-harmonizations. Thus religious humanism, language, a national musical style shaped by a national temperament, the method of performance, the general movement of European music away from the church modes towards clearly defined key—all exercised decisive pressures on the evolution of the chorale melodies. Furthermore, the deliberate creative intervention of Luther, Schein, Bach and others raises the question of the individual composer's place in the stream of musical tradition, belonging to it, drawing from it, and contributing to it.

These are some of the factors which control the development of musical tradition in general. Music is the most nearly autonomous of the arts. Many people, of whom I am one, have felt that the highest achievements of European music are those which are freest from extra-musical considerations: Bach's keyboard fugues, Mozart's piano concertos, Beethoven's last quartets. The history of European music can even be seen as what appears to be an autonomous process of self-evolution, proceeding by the successive exhaustion of techniques and styles and their replacement by new ones. The golden age of counterpoint reaches its apogee with Palestrina and Lassus, while underneath, as it were, a new style of tonal harmony and emotionally expressive monody is shaping itself and gradually triumphs as the old style declines. While the final long-lined, dense-textured masterpieces of the baroque were being written, the new thin, seemingly trivial sonata-style was being born which was to grow into the style of the Viennese classics. And so on. But this stream of evolution and renewal from music's own resources is nevertheless controlled, as the course of any stream is controlled, by natural conditions, physical conditions, the sort of conditions we have just been considering: language, religion, social and even political environment. You will understand therefore why in discussing national musical traditions, I shall not confine myself to talking about musical compositions. A people's composed music is only the final distillation of its *general* musical tradition.

The tradition will hardly ever be pure; indeed the constant process of cross-fertilization within a culture or between cultures is an indispensable condition of health. There have been cases of musical traditions hermetically sealed off by historical or geographical conditions—Russian music until nearly the end of the seventeenth century, Japanese music, with no more than minimal contacts with Korea and China from the ninth to the nineteenth or (effectively) the twentieth, to some extent the musics of North and South India—and in each instance the stream of evolution has flowed very sluggishly and poorly. In the normal course a healthy tradition simply draws into itself the foreign musician or the foreign elements, as French music did Lully or as German Lutheran music did Catholic plainsong, and flows on enriched by them. In fact this ability to absorb without becoming saturated is one of the surest indexes of a country's musical well-being. I cannot completely endorse Bernard Shaw's sweeping dictum in his obituary article on Verdi that 'the anxious northern genius is magnificently assimilative: the self-sufficient Italian genius is magnificently impervious'.[7] The first half of the proposition is true enough; from Schütz and Bach to Wagner, Strauss and Henze, German composers have assimilated Italian and other elements, yet remained essentially German. But the Italians have not always been magnificently impervious. Verdi may have assimilated nothing from Wagner (which is the point Shaw wanted to make) but he certainly assimilated something from French grand opera. And Puccini and the lesser masters of *verismo* assimilated from both Wagner and even Debussy elements that enriched them without in the least diminishing their essential Italianate quality.

The factors of language, social environment and so on which I have mentioned as determinants of national musical tradition are, so to speak, inert factors. They define the conditions within which it develops but they are not, or only in limited ways, propellants. The active factor in a healthy musical tradition is the mutual influence of musicians and their public, a continuous interplay that is vital to its sustenance and development. When we say that Italy has 'an operatic tradition' we mean not only that opera began in Italy and that Italian composers have always played a leading part in opera composition and written a vast number of operas; we mean that the Italian public has for centuries had an insatiable appetite for opera. The public a composer needs may not be an enormously wide one like that. It may be quite small, a Renaissance court or a cultural élite of some other kind, in which case it may suffice in itself if the composer's music is excessively refined or intellectual. But it can also function, and in later times it nearly always has functioned, as a dynamic nucleus acting on the generally rather inert mass of the wider public and in some measure acting as intermediary between the composer and the bigger public. But a public of some sort must exist for the composer to interact with, if he is to be really fertile. It is difficult to believe that the wonderful outpouring of the German masters of the nineteenth and early twentieth centuries, particularly in the fields of solo song, piano music and chamber

---

[7] *The Anglo-Saxon Review*, March, 1901. Reprinted in *Shaw on Music* (ed. Eric Bentley) (New York, 1955), p. 146.

music, could have occurred in a country that lacked a large music-loving and music-performing public. Even a composer who writes *against* such a public, as Schoenberg did, is stimulated by its hostile reaction, by the sense that it is worth conquering and can be conquered. He is fertilized by it, while the music of composers working in isolation, with almost complete disregard of their public or for nothing more than their own satisfaction, like Skryabin or Ives, is essentially auto-erotic.

Because he failed to recognize the existence of such a public in England and was evidently ignorant of the existence of Dunstable, Byrd, and Purcell, a German journalist, Oscar Schmitz, published in 1918 a book about England with the title *The Land without Music*. There are no lands without music. I reject altogether the concept that some peoples are inherently 'more musical' or 'less musical' than others. Some, as I have said, have been sealed off by geography or history, and all nations have their ups and downs in the arts and in literature just as they have their vicissitudes of political power and fortune. The English had their ups musically from the eleventh century—I reckon from the Winchester Troper at Cambridge, which is the earliest extant manuscript of music written in parts anywhere outside treatises—to the end of the seventeenth; and after that they had a very long down. We tend to think of the Italians as outstandingly musical, yet in the early sixteenth century most of the important musical posts in Italy were filled not by natives but by men who are usually described as Netherlanders, who came from what is now Belgium and north-eastern France, whose native language was generally French though sometimes Flemish. It was they, if anyone, who were the 'most musical' people of late medieval Europe, but it is not easy to think of any very outstanding composer from that part of the world between Sweelinck and César Franck. Side by side with Italy, our grandfathers would have unhesitatingly put Germany. Yet already, although the Germans are still a great musical nation, one cannot help feeling that the heyday of German music—at any rate, the heyday of German musical creativity—is over. And throughout the Middle Ages the Germans played quite an insignificant part in the concert of Europe.

The reasons for these rises and declines of musical pre-eminence and the reasons why various countries have developed dissimilar musical traditions are subjects I want to examine more closely. I shall not say very much about America specifically because, historically, America—both Anglo-Saxon and Latin—belongs almost completely to the Western tradition. I have not forgotten African America and I have not forgotten jazz, which has now for half a century been gradually assimilated to the Western tradition while at the same time it maintains a separate existence. But I am not sure to what extent jazz can be considered truly African. Its rhythms, novel as they once were and seminal as they have been in Western music, are jejune by comparison with those of the complicated percussive counterpoint recorded by A. M. Jones in his *Studies in African Music*.[8] Nor have I forgotten American Indian music and its employment by composers as diverse as MacDowell and Busoni, Villa-Lobos, Carlos Chávez and Ginastera. These experiments in cross-fertilization are bound to be fruitful in time, when they have become a natural process rather than a somewhat artificial one.

[8] Two vols. (New York and London, 1959).

II

THE DYNAMIC SYNTHESIS

The fallacy that music is a 'universal language' is very popular and very beguiling. All the same it is a fallacy. It is not too difficult for a European or American to find pleasure in the actual sounds of many Asian musics. Then, led on by enjoyment, he can go on to study them—their instruments, their scale-systems, their literary contacts and their meanings—even perhaps learn to perform them. His mind grasps, his ears are pleased. But I suspect that, except for a few specially gifted spirits, the true ethos remains unperceived; the achievement of full perception is hardly demonstrable and those who think they have it will be hard to convince that they haven't. Even within the limits of our own most familiar Western classics, have we not all heard performers who can give skilful and polished performances that none the less demonstrate very imperfect ability to grasp the real ethos of Bach or Beethoven?

Aesthetic ethos is the end-product of tradition at a given time, and the longer and more complex the tradition, the more profound and subtle is the ethos. The ethos of Russian music is not too difficult for any European to grasp almost completely; its tradition has been short and uncomplicated and some of the most important strands in it come from our common Western tradition. Yet our grasp is not *quite* complete. Russian music is so easy to 'appreciate'; it seems so transparent; but it does not mean to us quite what it means to a Russian. I doubt whether any non-Russian has ever understood the hyperbole with which the most diverse Russian musicians have spoken of Glinka; we may hear a great deal in Glinka but we cannot quite bring ourselves to speak of him in the same breath with Beethoven, as Chaykovsky did. And this is not cultural chauvinism or national pride, or whatever one likes to call it, on the part of the Russians. It is, I believe, only an exaggerated expression of what people mean when they say that only an Austrian can completely understand Bruckner or a Frenchman Fauré. The rest of us hear the sounds but not all the overtones and under-tones.

The ethos of Western music generally has been produced by the longest and most complex continuously active musical tradition in human history. We know of no other musical tradition that is, in Kantian terms, a 'dynamic synthesis' spread over a thousand years. The basic substance in this synthesis was unquestionably the plain-song of the Roman Church, just as the core of all European thought and art was for many centuries those of the Church. The unification of the Latin liturgy and the music associated with it, under the Carolingian Empire, was not total; but the surviving pockets of Ambrosian chant in Italy, the lesser, accidental territorial variants of so-called Gregorian chant itself (such as the Sarum Use in England), even the much greater variant of Mozarabic chant sealed off in Spain under Moorish rule, were only dialects of a single language that was as universal as the Latin tongue itself among all cultured Europeans. Its basic melodic patterns were of the same kind and the associations they carried with them were the same. Even its earliest steps in evolution, the introduction of trope and sequence, and (more important) the beginnings of the vital development, polyphony, in organum and motet, were the same. That is to say, they originated in France and spread quickly along the great pilgrimage route to Northern Spain, to England and other lands nearer France, and with considerable time-lag to more distant ones. *Ars nova*, for instance, did not reach the Western Slavs—the Czechs and Poles—until the beginning of the fifteenth century, nearly a hundred years late and at a time when it was exhibiting strong symptoms of decadence in the country of its origin.

We do not know, though we can sometimes guess at, the nature of the various impacts on the universal European musical idiom by popular music in different countries, but (as I hope to make clear later) the rise of the vernacular languages to the status of literary languages in each country did make a considerable impact. It was probably the strongest factor of all in the diversification of the common Western musical idiom. Diffusion of a culture inevitably leads to diversification for many reasons: different social conditions and demands, political pressures and even what one might consider political accidents. Even types of notation soon tended to take on peculiar forms in different countries: the notation of Italian *ars nova*, the German *Hufnagelschrift*, the rhomboid Czech neumes of the fourteenth century. Nevertheless Italian music or French or German or English music as they emerged and gradually took on clearer definition were, and still are—as North American music is—no more than dialects of the general Western language, a language which is indeed international, though far from universal. Its melodic and rhythmic patterns in general carry the same associations for all of us. Harmonic tensions or asperities induce very much the same feelings in all of us. Subtle overtones of association are special to national groups, but there are innumerable conventions—some quite arbitrary, some resting on perceptible analogy (from the association of pitch with height, to the association of 6/8 time at a certain pace with the pastoral)—which convey the same meaning to all of us. They would not convey it, or perhaps any other meaning, to a Chinese or a Central African, but then African drum-rhythms would not convey any message to us.

These sound-symbols of Western music are the audible phenomena of a common ethos, an ethos which is less instinctive and intuitive than the Asian. It seems highly probable that this was not always so. It seems clear not only that early Christianity embodied many oriental elements, but that its music, through its Jewish origins, were also close to oriental types of music. To this day Gregorian chant, despite all the changes of interpretative style to which it has been subjected, has preserved something of the hypnotic, timeless, endlessly flowing property that is the essence of so much Asian music. But the stream of tradition, guided by different social and other conditions, has carried Western music in another direction and not only diffused and diversified it but fundamentally modified its ethos in harmony with the development of a religion and cultures increasingly foreign to those of the East. Greek thought and Roman materialism have wrought deep changes in us, changes that became much more visible as we gradually emerged from the Middle Ages and our God-centred world became more and more a man-centred world. The failure to consolidate a new Western Empire that should be Holy as well as Roman, the gradual replacement of Latin by the vernacular languages, the emergence of nation-states instead of patrimonial, feudal states, above all the Reformation: all these were main steps in the process that led through national consciousness to individual consciousness. In the course of this process we observe the emergence of the artist whose name was generally known and remembered, in place of the quasi-anonymity of the early Middle Ages, though it was very long before music was reduced to a language in which the musician conveyed not simply generalized emotions but his personal emotional experiences to his listeners. That had to wait until the romantic age. But long before this stage was reached, Western music had acquired an ethos far indeed from the Eastern, and the gap is so wide that it can be bridged —if it is bridgeable—only by a vast spiritual and intellectual effort. That so many attempts are now being made to bridge it, from both sides, is a most welcome development. The Western world has far too long arrogated music to itself, as if no other music were worthy of consideration; study of other musics may, at the very least, lead to some measure of appreciation and understanding though I doubt whether it will ever take us to the heart of the matter. The merely dialectal differences within the Western tradition are much less; in fact they demand less conscious effort to overcome them than the differences of historical period. All the same, they exist and we cannot always achieve total apprehension. I want to examine a little more closely how they came into existence and how they were modified by the processes of inbreeding and cross-breeding.

* * *

We are confronted by tangibles and intangibles. The most tangible pieces of evidence are instruments: remains of actual instruments, pictures of instruments and descriptions of instruments. But even from the dimmest ages—whether human culture arose in one centre and was diffused, or whether it arose independently in different centres—man found everywhere the materials for making the same general types of sound-producing agent: resonant surfaces of wood or skins to strike, stretched strings of animal gut or other substance to pluck or stroke with another stretched string (the string of the hunter's bow), pipes to be blown into, and the ideas of having several pipes or strings of different pitch or modifying the pitch of one pipe or string—all these are so widespread that they appear to belong to all musical cultures. Even some of their improved forms are universal: for instance the multiplication of plucked strings which we know as the harp was common to the earliest known cultures of Central Africa and Northern Europe, the Middle East and the Far East. Not only was the instrument with two reed-pipes which the Greeks knew as the *aulos* practically universal; the idea of providing it with a wind-chest and so producing the bagpipe is extremely widespread.

But one improved form was *not* common to the entire human race. Whether or not the idea of providing panpipes with a wind-chest was evolved by a Hellenistic Greek, the result—which we know as the organ, '*the* instrument' *par excellence*—seems to have been developed only in Europe. It is probably true to claim that technical ingenuity is a major part of the European inheritance from Rome, and considerable technical ingenuity was required to devise both means of maintaining wind-pressure other than by blowing into a bag compressed by the arm, and also a way of blowing into one of a number of pipes without moving the mouth along. The earliest organ of which anything survives is the early third-century one at Aquincum, the Roman city that stood near the site of modern Budapest; it is very small—you could stand it on your coffee-table—but it has all the essentials of a modern organ, including the rudiments of a keyboard. *That* is the first specifically European instrument.

Indeed all keyboard instruments are peculiarly European. We cannot do much more than speculate about the evolution of the organ during the seven centuries between the Aquincum instrument and that fabulous, often mentioned tenth-century organ in Winchester Cathedral with its four hundred pipes, though we read of

Charlemagne's gift of an organ to Pepin the Short and of Louis the Pious having one built in his palace at Aix-la-Chapelle. Perhaps the main feature of its early development was in size, from a little chamber-instrument useful for supporting voices in a limited space to something capable of filling the seemingly limitless space of a Gothic cathedral. It is surely not mere coincidence that the earliest known English polyphony, the two-part music of the Winchester Troper, appeared at the same place and nearly the same time as that famous organ, and that the earliest continental polyphony—the name of which is so mysteriously connected with the organ—should also have been developed in the great cathedrals and abbeys that were going up on the banks of the Seine and the Eure and the Vienne.

I shall have to return later to the role of the organ and instruments generally in the development of sophisticated polyphony, in which lies the most profound distinction between European and non-European musics. However, I think we may accept that while during the first millennium Western Christendom achieved a musical near-unity corresponding to its religious-liturgical unity but still recognizably related to non-European musics—for instance, in its structure by melodic formulae—one part of Europe now took a step which directed European music on to a widely divergent course that was to carry it far away from all others. It was to give Europeans ways of apprehending music, ways of thinking about music, ways of thinking *in* music, which during nearly another millennium have become peculiar to their stock and to those who have been long and intimately associated with them. Other forms of music took shape in France: the songs of the goliards, the wandering scholars, the courtly art of the troubadours and *trouvères* which thrust out across Europe and inspired imitation by the *Minnesänger* in Germany, while its musico-poetic forms influenced those of Italy and Spain, even some Middle English songs. Yet, although it is unsafe to say that anything in art is totally without after-effect, the monodic art of these poet-musicians seems to have made only an infinitesimal contribution to the European tradition; it was music for too enclosed a social circle—most of the practitioners were aristocrats—and connected with too limited a circle of artificial concepts. It merely passed like a meteor across the medieval sky. The steady light which illuminated European music more and more brilliantly came from polyphony, which—whether sacred or secular —was practised almost exclusively by churchmen. It is not too much to say that, however beautiful *trouvère* art and its kind were in themselves, they contributed to the European tradition only when they became polyphonic as they did in certain *conductus* with new, Latin texts and with Machaut, who was both a belated *trouvère* and a churchman.

The earliest appearance of national dialect in the central polyphonic tradition occurred in England and Italy. (The Germans seem to have known little or nothing about polyphony before about 1400, though there does exist a single isolated motet with French and German words, 'Brumas e mors, Brumas ist tot', from an earlier period.) The beginnings of Italian polyphony are still rather obscure. It may have been an offshoot of the main, French tradition, as English polyphony unquestionably was, and the early examples from Padua published by Giuseppe Vecchi in 1954[1] give some support to that view; yet when a piece suggesting French influence appears in mid-*trecento* Florentine music,[2] it stands out sharply from its surroundings. The remarkable feature of early Italian polyphonic music was the rapidity with which it developed peculiar characteristics, of which the most striking was the exuberant exploitation of vowels, in one part at a time, in secular compositions, as in this madrigal by the fourteenth-century Florentine, Giovanni da Cascia:[3]

---

[1] *Uffici drammatici padovani* (Florence, 1954), pp. 145–60.

[2] e.g. the Credo by Bartholus de Florentia in *The Music of Fourteenth-Century Italy*, I, ed. Pirrotta, (American Institute of Musicology, 1954), p. 1, and the virelai 'Je porte amiablement' by Donatus de Florentia, ibid., III (1962), p. 42.

[3] *The Music of Fourteenth-Century Italy*, I, p. 24.

Ex. 9

This exploitation of vowels is a very good example of the influence of a language on the development of a national style; extended vocal melismata have always been an outstanding characteristic of Italian music and can usually be traced to Italian influence when they appear in the music of other European countries. Another striking feature of early Italian polyphony is the employment of chromatic alteration, not only notated in the music itself but discussed—somewhat wrongheadedly—by the theorist of the period, Marchettus of Padua. This Italian art reached its apogee with Francesco Landini and then almost disappeared, gradually submerged under a wave of French influence probably emanating from the Papal court at Avignon and reaching tidal-wave proportions when the Popes returned to Rome after the Council of Constance. But it did not disappear without a trace. One of the earliest of the North European musicians who came flooding into Italy and occupied most of the important musical posts for a century or more, Ciconia of Liège, composed madrigals and *ballati* in the Italian style in the 1390s, though he wrote isorhythmic motets and Mass-fragments in the North European tradition when he was at Padua in later years. And the other newcomers, from Dufay onward, certainly absorbed Italian elements. The Italian tributary thus contributed to the main European tradition until, as we shall see, after a century or so it became by its power and volume the main stream itself.

In the meantime England also had made her contribution. One part of it was a purely technical device, the frequent exchange of phrases between voices. More important were the relative simplicity of the rhythms of English music and that predilection for thirds and sixths in the harmony which has often been commented on. Here is an example of typical English polyphony, probably about half a century later than Example 9; it is an anonymous Credo from the Old Hall manuscript:[4]

Ex. 10

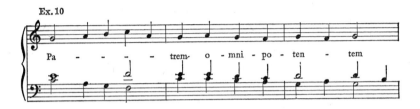

These English traits, rhythmic simplicity and euphonious thirds and sixths, persisted with the conservatism which has always been typical of English music, until the early part of the fifteenth century, while French *ars nova* reached a degree of rhythmic complexity which European music did not achieve again until five centuries later with *The Rite of Spring*.

Then in the first quarter of the fifteenth century something very remarkable occurred: one of those non-musical accidents of history which, like the exile of the Papacy to Avignon and its return to Rome, exercised a decisive influence on the tradition of European music. Throughout the Middle Ages English and French culture were in constant contact; an English musician would employ a peculiarly

---

[4] *The Old Hall Manuscript*, II, ed. Ramsbotham, Collins, and Hughes (Burnham, 1935), p. 1.

French technique such as isorhythm; but hitherto the French had been the dominant, the English the subsidiary culture. The historical accident was the triumph of English arms at the Battle of Agincourt in 1415 which made an English king heir to the throne of France and took there with him the members of the Chapel Royal—including composers whose work figures prominently in the Old Hall manuscript. More important: Henry V soon died, leaving as Regent of France his brother, the Duke of Bedford, who had in his service the greatest English composer before the Elizabethans, John Dunstable. During the period 1422–35 the Regent Bedford was in the closest contact, as ally and brother-in-law, with a prince whose subjects included the great majority of the most gifted musicians in Europe: the Duke of Burgundy. The ultimate consequence of that contact between the over-refinement of French *ars nova*, already modified by Italian contacts, and the simplicity and euphony of the English style are abundantly displayed in the music of the Franco-Flemings from Dufay and Binchois down to Josquin and his successors, that is to say in the main stream of the European tradition. Not only is the circumstantial evidence obvious in their compositions; we have the often quoted words of a poet at the Burgundian court, Martin le Franc, who wrote, in his *Le Champion des dames, c.* 1440, of Dufay and Binchois that

> . . . ilz ont nouvelle pratique
> De faire frisque concordance. . . .
> Et ont prins la contenance
> Angloise et ensuy Dunstable,
> Pour quoy merveilleuse plaisance
> Rend leur chant joyeux et notable.

Not long after that, the expulsion of the English armies from France was completed; only Calais remained for a century or so in English hands; and it is an ironic reflection that the only enduring consequence of Henry V's military triumphs was a major modification of the course of European music.

This may be a pleasant thought for those of us who believe in the superiority of cultural values to merely political ones, but we must not lose sight of the fact that the course of culture *was* affected by political—military—events, and it is worthwhile, indeed it is necessary, to pause here and consider how at this period, the heyday of the Renaissance, the development of music was affected in various parts of Europe by political events, even (perhaps particularly) by changes of dynasty. The main tradition was geographically diffused and locally modified, while at the same time countries which had hitherto shared freely in it found themselves partially excluded and thrust on a semi-independent course by events which had no obvious relationship to music. England was a case of the latter kind. Having made the first of her two major contributions to the European musical tradition, she found herself for a time more isolated from it than ever before. Not only was she shut off from France; the turmoil of the ensuing Wars of the Roses contributed to her cultural isolation, and, as the compositions of the Eton Choirbook bear witness, English music pursued a course of its own, almost completely ignoring the techniques of the Netherlands mainstream. It is true there were English composers such as Robert Morton and in all probability Walter Frye at the Burgundian court, but they were expatriates. The last Plantagenet and earliest Tudor composers were not conservative; they developed a florid and complicated style which has been compared with that of late English Gothic architecture, but it was a peculiar style and some of its features persisted in English music long after England had regained contact with the European mainstream.

In Bohemia political events first strengthened the Czech connection with the main European tradition and then strained it severely. The accession of the Luxembourg dynasty brought French influence to Prague. (It actually took Machaut to Prague for a short time as King John's secretary and possibly, but improbably, to the Polish court at Cracow in later years.) But the weakness and bad faith of John's grandsons in allowing Jan Hus to be seized and burned by the Council of Constance led not only to a series of wars between Hus's followers and the Catholics, and then between different Hussite factions, but to peculiar developments in Czech music. For the Hussites were fanatical puritans in many respects and they condemned polyphony as a 'frivolous assault on the ears, an empty pastime'. On the other hand the Hussite movement produced a vast quantity of monophonic religious song, often polemic or warlike, which was to influence a great deal of later Czech music and even left its mark on the early Lutheran chorale. And in more than one respect the Hussite schism was the overture to that much wider musical schism, or series of schisms, produced by the Reformation.

The relationship of the Germans to the main tradition is particularly interesting. Even the technique of polyphony seems to have reached them only with Oswald von Wolkenstein and Hermann, the 'Monk of Salzburg', and for a hundred years or so they employed it mainly for the treatment of vernacular song on a modest scale in organ transcriptions and the so-called *Tenorlieder*. The Buxheim organ-book is evidence that the Western style had arrived by the middle of the fifteenth century, but its contents show a dichotomy: transcriptions of mostly Burgundian compositions on the one hand and settings of German songs on the other. Franco-Flemish music swamped Germany down to the beginning of the sixteenth century as it swamped Italy during the same period, yet before it had struck roots there long enough to produce anything that can really be called a tradition it was met by the Reformation with its fresh upsurge of German song, immensely strengthened by the new art of printing. Even dynastic changes probably had some influence on the course of events. We cannot attribute the Netherland musical conquest of Germany to the Habsburg acquisition of the Netherland dominions of Burgundy, but one of the consequences was certainly the attraction of Netherland musicians such as Isaac and Adam Rener to Austria, just as at the other end of Europe another ramification of Habsburg marriages carried the *capilla flamenca*, the 'Flemish chapel', of the Emperor Charles V to Spain where it put out of fashion the more specifically Spanish religious music of Anchieta and others that had been encouraged by Ferdinand and Isabella.

* * *

It is imperative to pause here and take stock. The pattern of the

European tradition had by this time, the early sixteenth century, become so rich and complex that even by making rather sweeping generalizations, as I have already been obliged to do, it is increasingly difficult to give an accurate impression of it. And this is a convenient place to pause, for even more profound changes than those wrought by the Reformation and the advent of printing had begun to affect the ethos of European music. In any discussion of music it is fatally easy to talk about techniques and forms, instruments and notation, which are the tangible aspects of music, and to lose sight of the indwelling spirit which is often so terribly difficult to convey in words, which can be truly conveyed only *in* music. Musical tradition is transmitted and constantly transmuted in terms of styles and technical procedures; and we can with some confidence trace these changes, subtle and complicated as they have often been, in an unbroken line from plainsong and organum down to our own day. But it is far more difficult to trace the indefinables and imponderables of which these styles and techniques are the audible phenomena. The mathematical and metaphysical intellections of music were not peculiar to the Western tradition; they were adopted by Arab theorists of the Middle Ages as happily as by Europeans, but they are a part of our tradition and have never been totally forgotten. There had long been a God-centred conception of religious music which even admitted the belief that the corpus of Gregorian chant had been dictated to Gregory the Great by the Holy Ghost—there are a number of medieval pictures of the Holy Ghost in the form of a dove actually doing it—and which regarded polyphony as essentially an adornment of the sacred object. But this God-centred conception gave way during the Renaissance to a man-centred conception. The plainsong *cantus firmus* was no longer a sacred object to be adorned; it was simply a constructional device and could by now be replaced by a secular *cantus firmus*. Yet while a profane theme could be sanctified by being put to a religious use, the reverse was by this period, if not utterly unthinkable, certainly shocking. And this also has lived on in our tradition; Bach thought nothing of turning secular music to account in a religious work, but he never adapted an aria or chorus from a church cantata in a secular one. I suspect that even in early nineteenth-century Paris, Berlioz's introduction and caricature of the 'Dies irae' in the *Symphonie fantastique* seemed a good deal more shocking than it does to us.

The sixteenth century was man-centred in that even its religious music began to express a more personal attitude to God, an attitude that shows itself in the Lutheran chorale and in the Calvinist vernacular psalm-settings, in Archbishop Cranmer's demand 'for every syllable a note', and in the recommendations of the Commission of Cardinals at the Council of Trent for a simpler church music that did not obscure the words. The sixteenth century, the century from Josquin to Monteverdi, was a period in which music became as never before a medium of *deliberate* communication between man and God and, still more, between man and man. Precise communication necessitates some degree of definition in the medium, and music can achieve this only by marriage with words or by employing significant symbols, and the pages of sixteenth-century musical history are filled with accounts of both. At the least, music—whether religious or secular—was so made that the text was clearly audible. Frequently the music attempted to express the text, even details of the text, or to illustrate it symbolically. In the extreme case, as with the French *musique mesurée* or with the recitative invented by the members of the Florentine *Camerata*, the music was primarily a vehicle for the text or a means of intensifying it. Instead of the words being hardly more than the pretext, the opportunity, for the polyphonic *chanson* as in the fourteenth and fifteenth centuries, they began as early as the 1530s, the heyday of Pierre Attaingnant's publications in Paris, to control the music. And the means of communication before long became much more rarefied than the deliberate devices and symbols of the madrigalists: the pitch associations of height and depth, ascent and descent, of 'painful' chromaticism, and so on. The old associations of the modes must have long been obliterated in practice by the clutter of polyphony, but before long major and minor began to emerge and in time to trail their clouds of association, imperceptible for a while but always accumulating until now, a third of a millennium later, we cannot hear B minor without our subconscious being stirred by memories of the Kyrie of Bach's Mass, the first movement of the Unfinished Symphony, and Chaykovsky's *Pathétique*.

If the European tradition had hitherto been both unified and developed by the transmission of techniques, it was now unified by a common synthesis of tenuous associations and hardly definable meanings. It was also fascinatingly diversified within that unity by the dynamism of the often conflicting forces that continually acted upon each other. The detailed, circumstantial mapping of these forces and their interaction would be an operation of terrifying complexity; nevertheless if one stands back from the map of history and half closes one's eyes as one does before a large painting or tapestry, rich in detail, in order to eliminate what is subordinate, the grand general lines of the continuing tradition stand out.

The first thing one notices is that the heart of the tradition after the middle of the sixteenth century was no longer Franco-Flemish. Gradually the Netherlands ceased to participate actively in the propagation of the main tradition, except for the isolated case of Sweelinck who transmitted a partly English tradition of keyboard composition to Scheidt and the other North German organists. At the beginning of the sixteenth century the Netherlanders dominated everything; at the beginning of the seventeenth, after the deaths of Lassus and Philipp de Monte, they dominated nothing. Like the great political empires of history, the Netherland musical empire seems finally to have overstretched and exhausted itself. What had really happened was that the style it had perfected, through the techniques of imitative polyphony, had exhausted itself. The course of events is most clearly traceable in the land where the hegemony of the Netherlanders had been most striking: Italy. From Ciconia and Dufay onward, the Northerners who visited Italy were infected by Italianism, by Italian cantilena and Italian directness and simplicity. (I hesitate to mention the frottola, because much of the spirit and the technical characteristics of the frottola were hardly peculiar to Italy; but the dissemination of the frottola by printing, through the near-monopoly of music-printing enjoyed by Venice at the beginning of the sixteenth century, gave it a special advantage.)

The many Northerners who settled in Italy became even more Italianized though they transmitted Netherland techniques to their pupils. Willaert and de Rore are typical figures. The conservative church music of the Roman school and the progressive, almost dramatic church music of the Venetian school, were alike Netherland in origin but Italian in fulfilment. The Italian madrigal was created mainly by Frenchmen and Flemings—Verdelot and Arcadelt—though it grew from the frottola, and it reached its apogee and its decadence with Italians: Marenzio, Monteverdi, Gesualdo. And the change of taste which was to make the contrapuntal styles seem old-fashioned—the half-declamatory, half-coloratura monody and vocal duet, opera, the instrumental monody and duet which were to lead to the sonata—this was Italian, too: a triumph of Italian song and sense of drama over the last relics of Netherland art.

The Italian continuation of the old Franco-Flemish tradition dominated Europe from the middle of the sixteenth century. The music of the Spaniard Victoria is hardly distinguishable from that of the Roman school. German composers like Hassler and Schütz went to Venice to study with the Gabrielis. The Polish king, Sigismund III, invited Marenzio to his court at Warsaw and initiated a whole line of Italian musicians, including Giovanni Francesco Anerio, as masters of the Polish Chapel Royal; at the same time native Polish composers tried to emulate the splendours of the Venetian poly-choral style, and thus made a splash whose faint ripples reached Russia around 1700.[5] English church-music escaped Italian influence, owing to the religious situation, and cultivated a rough but vigorous dialect of the older Netherland style. So did the English part-songs of Byrd, so often mis-called madrigals. But the true English madrigal of Morley and the younger men, with all its sub-varieties of ballet and canzonet, was quite frankly modelled on the Italians. The French polyphonic *chanson* was influenced by, as in early days it had influenced, the Italian madrigal.

Yet by this time one can distinguish more and more clearly those traits we can recognize as markedly French. I shall return later to the particularly close relationship of French melody to text, to the

[5] See p. 47 below.

words themselves and not simply to the emotion they convey. I shall also draw attention to the fact that French instrumental music is seldom absolute music. When French music is not controlled by a text, it is still frequently controlled by extra-musical ideas or by intellectual concepts. I am naturally aware that the same might be said of a great deal of non-French music, but the French cannot point, as the Italians or Germans can, to a vast treasure of absolute music in addition. These traits are apparent as early as the fourteenth century; there is a *chace* in the Ivrea manuscript describing a hawking scene, which is tightly constructed—a three-part canon—which yet carries naturalistic representation of the words (hunters' cries and so on) to a degree never surpassed, if it was reached, in the later Italian *cacce* on the French model; one might put it that in this case the French *chace* is 'less song' than the Italian *caccia*. So in the sixteenth century, as French music began to establish its own identity a little apart from the Italian-dominated main stream, the Parisian *chanson* was not only programmatic, as with Jannequin, but more syllabic. Similarly the church music of Antoine Brumel is much more syllabic than that of his colleagues in Italy. And then when the Italians invented opera and promptly separated the wheat from the chaff, the aria from the recitative, they were followed by all Europe except France, which through Lully, Rameau and the French operas of Gluck, developed her own operatic tradition, the essence of which was the translation into music of French classical tragedy.

The mainstream of Western music in the seventeenth century flowed through opera, cantata (a thin slice of opera removed from the stage to the salon), and sonata (which was the instrumental counterpart of the cantata). In the eighteenth century opera threw off the independent orchestral *sinfonia* as a byproduct. These forms were all Italian in origin and, except the symphony, long practised mainly by Italians. The *concertato* style and the *basso continuo* technique both originated in Italy. Italian performers carried Italian music to every part of Europe, and foreign composers, even if they did not actually go to Italy to study, made no secret of the fact that they were imitating Italian styles. Purcell claimed that in his sonatas he had 'faithfully endeavour'd a just imitation of the most fam'd

37

Italian Masters',[6] and Bach transcribed Vivaldi's concertos and took them as his models. Two of the greatest German composers of the eighteenth century, Handel and Mozart, wrote what one can only call sublimated Italian music; I will say nothing of Graun and Hasse and the Italian works of Gluck. Most of them learned something from France as well, but it was the Italian element that easily dominated the European tradition—and continued to play a leading role in opera until the death of Puccini.

* * *

In other fields it lost its pre-eminence earlier, first in the sphere of instrumental music and earliest of all in that variety which, being least songlike, is least suited to the Italian genius: music for keyboard. In the days of the early maturity of keyboard music—the drawing together of the resources and possibilities of polyphony under the hands of one performer, the peculiarly Western kind of music on an exclusively Western instrument—Italian masters from Cavazzoni to Frescobaldi could hold their own with any. Later, despite such isolated masters as Scarlatti and Clementi, the keyboard seldom attracted the highest Italian talents, who found more congenial media in opera or violin music. In the North it was different and from the North came a tributary which ultimately grew in importance and poured into the European main stream with a force and volume that diverted it into fresh channels where the Italian contribution was no longer the predominant one. That tributary flowed first from England, with an early contribution in the form of a type of keyboard variation brought from Spain. (Incidentally, it was brought by a dynastic marriage, Philip II's with Mary I, and it was the only fruit of that marriage.) The techniques of English keyboard music, enriched and focused through Sweelinck, passed into the heritage of the North German organ-composers.

I am not suggesting that German instrumental music sprang entirely from the North German organists. German vernacular song, whether secular or in the form of the Lutheran chorale, is the

[6] Preface to the *Sonatas of III Parts* (London, 1683).

basis of the German tradition. Yet, despite the genius of Schütz and the great talent of others, Lutheran church music could never have been more than a national—I had almost said 'a provincial'—dialect. German keyboard music had been closely associated with German song from the early organ-tablatures onward and it was German keyboard music, particularly that of the North, nourished by the Protestant chorale, that first offered the German musician a medium and styles specially suited to his nature and through which he could achieve a widely comprehensible utterance. It lent itself to rich and complicated textures such as the German artist loves. (Consider the way in which, as Roger Fry pointed out in *Vision and Design*, Dürer inserted 'a mass of brilliant detail' in his pen-and-ink copies of engravings by Mantegna—or consider the score of *Heldenleben*.) Keyboard music was a medium for both imagination and thought *in terms of sound*. In the mid-eighteenth century its percussive, dynamic, affective potential was at last realized in the hands of C. P. E. Bach, and the sonata-style acquired a new dimension, a new depth, which was extended not only in the new instrument, the pianoforte, but in new instrumental combinations. The style and the media were both congenial to that quasi-metaphysical, quasi-dialectic thinking-in-sound (as distinct from the marrying of independent intellectual concepts with music) which produces music that seems not skilfully organized but a living, dramatically struggling organism. This surely is the major element in the German contribution to the Western tradition.

The chief glories of German music are commonly associated with Vienna; the Habsburg capital inexorably attracted musicians not only from all over Germany but from the other Habsburg lands and from Italy. Vienna was the main, though by no means the only, focus for the fusion of German with non-German traditions, and this natural fusion deeply enriched and seldom seriously weakened the German tradition. (Incidentally the Habsburgs were agents of diffusion as well as concentration. Their suppression of Czech national culture for more than two centuries after 1620 seriously weakened the indigenous Czech musical tradition but fruitfully scattered some of the best Czech musicians all over Germany—for

39

instance, to Mannheim—and as far afield as Paris and London.) But the cosmopolitan, Italianized ambience of the Imperial court was not the 'real' Germany. It is in North and North Central Germany, Protestant Germany, that we find most of the origins of the essentially German elements in the first place, and it was from North Germany and Saxony that came Handel and the Bachs, Beethoven and Weber, Mendelssohn and Schumann, Brahms and Wagner.

I think it is hardly an exaggeration to claim that the role of the keyboard in the development of German music is comparable with that of the human voice in Italian music. Most of the composers I have just mentioned, and Mozart among the South Germans, were eminent performers on keyboard instruments, and the piano and its idioms lie at the heart of very much of their music. When the piano is directly involved it plays a dominant role, as in Schumann's songs where the piano-part is often almost a self-contained entity. When the piano is not directly involved, as in Schumann's string quartets, Mendelssohn's chamber-music, and Brahms's work in general, its presence is nevertheless immanent. So it is frequently in Beethoven: the duet 'Namenlose Freude' in *Fidelio* is curiously pianistic and I suggest that the sketchy texture of the last quartets, where more is implied than is actually sounded, derives ultimately from the texture of piano music which is a constant compromise between real and implied sound. One might write a long chapter, if not a whole book, on the triangular relationship between the piano, romanticism, and the German character.

Despite the active musical life of Germany after the Thirty Years War, it was (I think) not until the eighteenth century that Europe in general became conscious of it as a great new force—first perhaps through Handel, a real Saxon in origin and training, no matter how Italianized later. Handel made his deepest impact in Italy and England, as the Mannheim symphonists did in France. Then with Bach's two most famous sons, Carl Philipp Emanuel and Johann Christian, Haydn, Mozart, and Beethoven, the ascendancy was unmistakable. But, despite Mozart's operas and *Fidelio* and Wagner, it was an ascendancy mainly in instrumental music. It is so recent that it blocks our backward view; it seems the greatest of all. And although its techniques are now outdated and the very bases of its ethos have long been questioned, if we open those half-closed eyes and peer into the great tapestry in all its detail, we can see how many German threads have gone into the pattern. We also see the infinite complexity of their interweaving with the Italian, the French, and those others from all over the Western world which have together created the great synthesis of our tradition.

III

THE HISTORICAL PROCESS AT WORK

Having attempted to take a mountain-top view of the evolution of the Western musical tradition with all its complications, I want now to examine a smaller and relatively simple field in more detail. In Europe one can never find an independent musical culture like that of Japan, for instance. It derived originally from China but, as I have already remarked, thanks partly to political isolation, partly to veneration for that which is old, types of Japanese music seem to have come down unchanged in essence for many centuries. As always, we must be cautious in making assumptions about music from times before it could be recorded in comprehensible notation. But it does appear likely that, for instance, the court music known as *gagaku* has survived for many centuries with no more changes, perhaps fewer, than the plainchant of the Roman Church has undergone during the same period. The most beautiful of all Japanese instruments, the *koto*, is said to have been introduced from China in the seventh century A.D.; its form is known to have undergone modifications but they cannot have been far-reaching like those of Western keyboard instruments; its repertory waited a thousand years after its arrival in Japan before it was enriched by Yatsuhashi's invention of a species of variation-composition. The more popular guitar-like *samisen* arrived, also from China, in the sixteenth century and to some extent supplanted the more ancient *biwa*. And so one could continue. It is a history as nearly uneventful as history can be. But the music was one that answered to the needs and temperament of the Japanese people: the aristocratic *gagaku*, the music of dances, of *no* plays and the *kabuki* theatre. It persisted until the arrival of European music in the very recent past, one consequence of which has been a determined attempt by Japanese composers to adopt and assimilate Western techniques, although up to the present they seem to be in the position of the Westerner fascinated by one or other of the musics of Asia or Africa; they have mastered the techniques but have naturally failed to grasp the ethos.

Even if it did not stand totally apart from the Western tradition, the history of Japanese music is so uneventful and so meagrely charted that it would not serve my purpose. Fortunately we can turn to another tradition that can be studied in near-laboratory conditions: a tradition with the same distant origins as that of the West, yet hermetically sealed off from it for long periods, a tradition in which the re-entry of Western elements took place so clearly and unmistakably, and is so well documented, that we can observe every detail of the process. The case I have in mind is Russian music which for many centuries was as hermetically sealed as Japan's but has now undergone nearly three hundred years of assimilation and development.

I have already shown how political and other non-musical factors can act upon musical tradition. In the early Middle Ages two issues of ecclesiastical politics were profound and far-reaching so far as music was concerned. One was the attempted, and nearly successful, unification of the Western liturgy and its music under the Carolingian Empire. The Eastern Church also systematized Byzantine chant, from which the Western chant probably proceeded, but it is characteristic of the difference between Western European and Middle Eastern cultures that the typical Western expansion and enrichment of the melodic canon was made by the interpolation of fresh melodic phrases, whereas the typical Eastern method was to elaborate and ornament the original phrases themselves: an attitude to melody that makes one think of still further Eastern musical cultures. (There are similar traits in the Mozarabic chant of medieval Spain.) It is also probable that the interdiction of chromatic intervals by the Fathers of the Church was less effective in the East.

A much deeper cleavage between the musics of the Eastern and Western churches was caused by the second of the ecclesiastical issues: the increasing tolerance of instruments in the music of the Roman Church while they continued to be forbidden, as they still are, by the Orthodox. The result is demonstrated most dramatically by Russia's centuries of exclusion from the common European musical culture in which the Western Slavs participated thanks to their adoption of Christianity in the Roman form. For the basis of this culture, that which distinguishes it most sharply from any other —this cannot be repeated too often—is its high development of polyphony; and the ever-increasing sophistication of Western polyphony is surely due to the fact that the human voice in its adventures in tonal space could rely on instrumental support. By this I mean something more than a fundamental pitch reference, a drone. The drone—including the sort of changing-pitch drone presumably supplied by the second pipe of the *aulos* and still supplied by the string *tâmbura* in Indian music—is no doubt one of the earliest forms of polyphony we know, probably the very earliest. In the West, single notes of the basic plainsong were vastly prolonged in drone-fashion in the twelfth-century Notre Dame *organa*. But the very word *organum*, much debated though its meaning has been, in itself most obviously indicates the participation of an instrument or instruments. (Not necessarily an 'organ', of course, any more than *biblion* meant a Bible.) Rude polyphony is not impossible without instrumental support, as we know from the primitive music of Malaysia and other countries, but it is significant that most even *very* primitive polyphony does involve instruments and I find it hard to believe that the continuous experimental evolution of Western polyphony would have been possible in a purely vocal art. With instrumental support—more than a drone, more than a tenor backbone —with a certain amount of actual instrumental doubling, the human voice could trace new kinds of interwoven line with confidence. Nor does it seem at all likely that secular polyphony would have developed very far without the ecclesiastical lead. The Church was paramount in medieval music as in art and letters; secular polyphony was nearly always composed by churchmen, who naturally modelled the secular motet on the sacred motet. When we come across an exception such as Adam de la Hale—and he was trained by the Cistercians in his youth—we find that the polyphony of his *rondeaux* is technically naïve by comparison with the motets of the earlier thirteenth century. Carried on the shoulders of churchmen—Philippe de

Vitry, Machaut, Dufay, Ockeghem, Josquin, and a host of others—Western polyphony constantly developed new techniques, and continues to do so.

The position was startlingly different in the lands where the Eastern Church forbade the participation of instruments. Up to the thirteenth century Russia, with Kiev as her political centre, belonged essentially to the European cultural area, though an outpost of it. She was politically and culturally and in religion the offspring of Byzantium instead of Rome, but there was nothing in the essential nature of Byzantine-derived chant that could have prevented its polyphonic elaboration on lines parallel with those of the West. There is even one isolated hint in an eleventh-century chronicle that Kievan Russia may have had some rudimentary secular polyphony. Throughout medieval Russia the professional secular musicians were the *skomorokhi*, the equivalents of the Western *jongleurs* and *Gaukler*, and like them they sang and played on instruments. In this chronicle there is an account of *skomorokhi* performing before Svyatoslav II, Prince of Kiev, 'some bringing forth the sounds of *gusli* (a very vague word at that period, though it was later applied to a kind of dulcimer), others singing organal sounds (*organïya glasï poyushche*)'.[1] I wish I knew precisely what the chronicler meant by that, but at any rate it does suggest some sort of polyphony involving instruments. Unfortunately the Orthodox clergy not only forbade the playing of instruments in church; they often succeeded in hounding the performers on these things of the Devil away from princely courts, so that the *skomorokhi* were reckoned among the dregs of society. (The *jongleurs* in the West were also ill-regarded by the Church, but this mattered much less since the Church itself cherished and developed the Western musical heritage.) It was only in the 'free' cities, above all in Novgorod which was an oligarchic republic right down to the time of Ivan the Terrible, that the *skomorokhi* were considered respectable and were able to organize themselves into guilds.

Novgorod also escaped the Tatar conquest which for two centuries

[1] Nikolay Findeïzen, *Ocherki po istorii muzïki v Rossii* (Moscow and Leningrad, 1928–9), I, p. 68.

cut off the greater part of Russia from its European contacts. But the very survival of Novgorod shows that we cannot blame 'the Tatar yoke' for the total stagnation of Russian music. The *skomorokhi* were not learned musicians, but Novgorod had an ecclesiastical song-school that was famous as early as the twelfth century and maintained its fame for four hundred years, until the Muscovite tsars carried off the best of its singers to establish their court chapel. Yet the Novgorod song-school did nothing for hundreds of years to develop polyphony; its only enrichment of traditional song was through elaboration of the single melodic line. And since, so long as music remains monodic there is no pressing reason why notation should indicate precise pitch, Russian notation remained neumatic for hundreds of years after the West had been obliged to adopt the staff.

It was not until the sixteenth century that Russian musicians were emboldened to take their earliest modest steps in polyphonic composition, writing two or three lines of carefully aligned neumes in *campo aperto*. In the seventeenth century they ventured on four-part composition, though still only in the form of very naïve note-against-note accretions to a *cantus firmus* in a middle part. These pioneers of Russian polyphony appear to have come from Novgorod, which was still Russia's point of contact with the West, and the resulting chords suggest that they had some knowledge of Western harmony. During the second half of the seventeenth century the Muscovite state acquired the Ukraine and entered into more amiable relations with Catholic Poland, which musically shared the general European tradition. From the Ukraine and Poland, Russia at last acquired the five-line staff and what was called 'Kiev part-singing', which was still a very simple three-part affair though more respectful of the conventions of Western harmony. Even this very simple polyphony aroused the hostility of the conservative Old Believers, who rejected all ecclesiastical reforms and all musical innovations.

*   *   *

The steps by which one culture begins to accept and absorb

another are always fascinating, and the case of Muscovite Russia, a European nation isolated from the rest of Europe by religion even more than by the years of Tatar domination, is a particularly rewarding one to study since it is so clear-cut. We can actually put our finger on the origins of the first Russian book of Western theory. It was written by a Kiev-born musician, Nikolay Diletsky, who studied with the Polish composer Mielczewski and significantly wrote his own *Gramatyka muzyczna* originally in Polish, though he settled in Moscow in 1681 and brought a Russian version of his book with him.[2] Diletsky seems to have had some knowledge of Zarlino, probably at second or third hand, but he evidently understood him very imperfectly. The nearest he gets to the concepts of major and minor is to say that 'ut-mi-sol is merry music, re-fa-la is woeful'. And when his disciples, Kalashnikov and Vasily Titov, embarked on the construction of elaborate 'spiritual concertos' in twelve, sixteen or even twenty-four parts, in crude imitation of Polish imitations of the Venetian polychoral style of a century earlier, they were again fatally handicapped by the want of instrumental support, not being allowed even a continuo bass. As for non-liturgical Russian music, well into the eighteenth century there was—other than folk-music— only one all-purpose type for secular songs, official acclamations of the monarch, psalms and other sacred songs for domestic use; it consisted of two voices, usually running in parallel thirds, above a bass which was certainly sometimes sung but may also in secular music have been played on an instrument—in fact a lay-out like that of the most primitive Italian trio-sonatas of a much earlier period.

Thus, right up to the first decades of the eighteenth century, thanks to the Church's ban on instruments, Russian music had failed to develop from its own resources any but the most primitive polyphony, and was crippled in its first faltering steps in the path of more elaborate Western music. It is true that *folk*-polyphony has flourished in both Russia proper and in the Caucasus, and if examples were known earlier than the nineteenth century they would be immensely impressive. But although it is known that exceedingly primitive peoples can achieve exceedingly primitive

[2] It was published by S. V. Smolensky (St. Petersburg) in 1910.

polyphony without outside help, there is (so far as I know) no evidence that Russian peasant part-singing pre-dates ecclesiastical part-singing. And whether or not this folk-polyphony, with its 'under-voices' branching out from the main melody and then re-joining it, is a homely imitation of church singing, it has played no part in the main tradition of Russian music. Composers have some-times noticed it, and sometimes imitated it to give a folkish flavour to an opera chorus, but nothing more. The later course of Russian music, indeed everything that most of us know and think of as Russian music, was the result of something imposed from outside, by a political factor. It was foreign. And although the old Russian element was assimilated into it, it was the foreign tradition that did the assimilating, whereas the attempt to assimilate psuedo-Italian techniques in Russian music around 1700 only led into a cul-de-sac.

It is hardly an exaggeration to say that until the middle of the eighteenth century Russia had almost no live and active musical tradition in the sense of a music handed down over a long period and gradually modified in the process of handing down, freely judged by the community and answering its needs. Ecclesiastical chant had developed away from Byzantine chant and been modified over the centuries—as we can gather from various accounts and from the imperfect notation (so far as it has been possible to read it)—yet it remained held within crippling limits which made free, natural development impossible. Moreover it contributed almost nothing, except a tradition of male vocal culture, to Russian music in general. It was barren. Later Russian music owes nothing to it but a few quotations, as in Rimsky-Korsakov's *Easter Overture* and the first movement of Chaykovsky's *Pathétique* Symphony. It provided equally barren soil for those first seeds of Western theory and tech-nique to fall on. Folk-music had gone its own way, as folk-music always does. It may well have been influenced by church music, and one modern Russian scholar, Maxim Brazhnikov, believes he has found traces of folk-influence on the church-music of the early seventeenth-century. But the hard fact is that, although the *words* of some Russian folk-songs suggest that they originated far back in pre-Christian times, we do not know what Russian folk-music was like until the middle of the eighteenth century. The first printed collection of 'Russian simple songs', Trutovsky's, began to appear in 1776. And what Trutovsky and his immediate successors noted down consisted largely of urban versions of peasant-transmitted folk-music; it was many years later still that research brought to light the pure peasant song which presumably preserves older forms, though we still do not know how much older.

*　　*　　*

Nothing in history begins on a blank page; everything is to some extent palimpsest. But the state of Russian music in the early eighteenth century was as near to *tabula rasa* as one can expect to find, and we can study every later layer as it was inscribed on it. The first important marks were made in the 1730s under the Empress Anna. They were all made by Italians: actors capable of performing musical intermezzi and a *commedia per musica*, instrumentalists and composers. It was a foreign culture, not absorbed naturally but imposed from the top as a belated consequence of the drastic Westernizing policy of Peter the Great. Peter himself had cared nothing for music, though he imported foreign—mostly German— oboists, trumpeters and drummers to play in and train bands for his new Western-model army, but what they played seems to have been limited to the primitive three-part music I have already described. And there had been two or three sporadic attempts, even under Peter's father, to give Western-style theatrical performances, sometimes with interpolated songs, under court auspices; but they had all fizzled out. Not so the Italian invasion that began in the 1730s, which was invited by the music-loving Anna and supported by a nobility who may or may not have been genuine lovers of Italian music but who no doubt loved fashion and the Empress's favour. This was a permanent invasion. Anna appointed a Neapolitan opera composer, Francesco Araja, as her *maestro di cappella*, and he stayed for a quarter of a century. The Venetian violinist-composer, Luigi Madonis stayed even longer. But although Madonis published violin sonatas in Petersburg and Araja ventured in 1755 to set a Russian libretto by a distinguished poet, Sumarokov, it can hardly be said that they contributed much or directly to the music of the Russian people. What they were doing was to condition a cultural élite to the enjoyment of sophisticated European music. They neither influenced nor, except in a few doubtful cases, were they influenced by, church music or folk-music. But aristocratic amateurs and literary men, such as Sumarokov himself, began to play the violin or clavichord and to sing songs with keyboard accompaniment. And the step from amateur performance to amateur composition was inevitable. Moreover in those days of serfdom a wealthy noble could maintain a private orchestra of his serfs—which in some cases took the form of that peculiar Russian institution, the horn band— or even send a specially gifted serf to Italy for a complete musical education. In fact the earliest professional Russian musicians of any distinction, such as the composer Yevstigney Fomin, were Italian-trained serfs. By the last quarter of the century, though hardly before, a really hybrid music began to emerge. Other foreign musicians came to Russia either as temporary visitors or to settle permanently: Germans, Czechs, Frenchmen whose *opéra comique*— favoured by Catherine the Great—supplanted Italian opera as the most fashionable form. And the newcomers wrote operas with Russian texts and sometimes on Russian subjects. Martín y Soler not only composed a Russian comic opera on a Russian subject but provided it with an overture based on folk-melodies.

The aristocratic dilettanti also began to take more interest in folk-music, perhaps as a result of the publication of Trutovsky's collection. They composed not only *romansï* in imitation of the *romances* of *opéra comique* but what they called 'Russian songs' in imitation of urbanized folk-song, and they wrote variations for piano on folk-tunes as well. In the theatre native composers would write *opéras comiques* with French texts for the Court, as Bortnyansky did, or provide Russian-style music (often merely harmonized folk-tunes) for lavish insertion in spoken Russian plays—especially plays introducing peasant characters—in the style of *opéra comique* or, still more perhaps, of English ballad opera. During this period of hybridization one major difficulty was the harmonization of folk-song. Both the published collections and the theatre music show considerable discomfort in the reconciliation of modal tunes with the conventional harmonic minor or major of Western music. This was a problem that worried Russian composers for many years and was finally solved by Glinka, Balakirev, Mussorgsky and their contemporaries, who tackled it quite empirically and with no pretensions to scholarship.

From roughly 1780 to 1860 Russian music—and now I mean Russian music in the broadest sense, not simply composition but the entire constitution of Russian musical life—presents a classic example of a music produced by well-defined circumstances, in which the social element was predominant. After Catherine the Great, who actually deigned to appear as the author of an opera-libretto on an historical Russian subject, there was no particular pressure from the monarchy. Nothing more than a little encouragement here or a little discouragement there, little suggestions which were naturally veiled commands—as when Nicholas I commissioned General Alexey Lvov to produce a Russian tune that could take the place of the British 'God save the King' (a commission which resulted in the melody 'Bozhe tsarya khrani' which appears at the end of the *1812* Overture), or when the same Emperor indicated to Glinka that it would be a pleasant idea to re-name his opera *Ivan Susanin* as *Life for the Tsar*. But then Nicholas's interest in the preservation of the monarch was very natural; any other ruler might have offered similar promptings. The initial impetus that brought European musical culture to Russia had come from the monarchy, which continued to foot the bill for the Imperial theatres in St. Petersburg and Moscow, and this of course included opera. But the driving force and the conditions now emanated from the aristocracy.

The aristocracy was as mixed in its motives as it had been under the Empress Anna, as mixed as any social group at any time: the deeply musical, the superficially musical, the mere followers of fashion. But there was a considerable leavening of genuine and intelligent music-lovers: the immortalized Count Razumovsky who maintained a string quartet while he was ambassador at the Imperial Court in Vienna; Prince Nikolay Golitsïn who also encouraged some quite memorable quartet-composition; General Alexey Lvov, violinist and composer of much more than the new national anthem; Prince Odoevsky, a man of all-round culture and composer of some really charming trifles; the brothers Count Michal and Count Mateusz Wielhorski, one a cellist, the other a composer. Among the untitled lesser nobility was Alexander Ulïbïshev, who wrote a famous book on Mozart and a notorious one on Beethoven, and encouraged the genius of the young Balakirev. These men were Maecenases of the best kind. They themselves performed and often composed. They maintained private orchestras and choirs, amassed considerable music libraries, and encouraged the visits to Russia of such distinguished foreign musicians as Liszt, Clara Schumann and Berlioz. The foreign musicians who actually stayed in Russia for longer periods in the nineteenth century were less distinguished; John Field and Adolf Henselt were the most notable. Most of those who played the leading professional roles in Russian musical life through this period—for instance, the Venetian opera composer Catterino Cavos—who directed opera in St. Petersburg for nearly forty years—were by European standards hardly third-raters; they would have left little mark on the pages of history if they had stayed at home.

This was a top-heavy and limited culture, resting on no broad national basis. The lower orders contributed to it nothing but tavern songs and gypsy songs that might be borrowed or imitated, and the middle class was so small as to be practically non-existent. (Even the lower ranks of the civil service, like the commissioned ranks of the army and navy, were filled by men who were technically of the 'nobility'.) It was a culture carried on by, and for, amateurs with the assistance of native and foreign professional mediocrities. In so far as it was creative, it produced the kinds of music such a society wanted—not something *better* than they wanted: opera, mostly written by the professionals; a great quantity of sentimental or 'Russian' or gypsy songs with piano; and salon music for piano, some of which is curious if not very valuable. (In this category I include the various funeral marches for fallen heroes of the war of 1812, composed by Prince Pavel Dolgoruky, and a 'novel in valses', *Quand j'étais jeune*, by one of the Titovs, a whole family of amateur composers whose best songs lived on for quite a long time.) Chamber music also was written by amateurs and commonly took the form of occasional compositions for oddly constituted groups of the composer's friends; it frequently failed to rise above the level of serenades or *divertissements* on operatic airs. Orchestral music was little cultivated by the amateurs, and this is not at all strange when one considers how much practical knowledge is needed to write for orchestra. It is true a dilettante who had composed a polonaise or an opera could turn to a professional to orchestrate it for him, but few of either class commanded the skill to construct an extended instrumental piece of the symphonic type. And they had no strong inducement to do so.

It would be going too far to say that Russia had no orchestras. There were the private orchestras of the nobility, probably smaller and decidedly less competent than the one Haydn had directed for the Esterhazys; there was a court orchestra; and Petersburg actually had a Philharmonic Society with an orchestra consisting partly of foreign players from the Opera, partly of the wealthy amateurs who ran the Society in order to give themselves opportunities to perform rather than to provide concerts for the public. In 1850 a Concert Society was founded for 'the propaganda of classical music in the best possible performance'. There was no active, healthy public concert life like that of Vienna and Paris and London, no regular concerts directed and performed by first-rate professional musicians like the Philharmonic Society's concerts in London or the Conservatoire concerts in Paris. There was no public demanding symphonic music, no fine orchestra eager to play it. Consequently none was written, even when a composer appeared who could have written it.

*　　*　　*

For out of all this dilettantism and mediocre professionalism, these foreign art-forms assimilating the music of the common people, a tradition did emerge. It grew and matured as traditions do, and after half a century showed signs of fertility. I shall consider later the whole question of the relation between tradition and the individual talent; at this point I need only make the fairly obvious remark that natural talent benefits enormously if it springs up in the fertile soil of an established tradition. Certainly in the 1830s Russia began to throw up musicians better equipped technically and more naturally gifted than their predecessors had been. One of these was Alyabyev, who is best known by Liszt's brilliant transcription of one of his songs; he was a talented and quite prolific composer whose E minor Symphony is one of the earliest Russian symphonies. Another was Verstovsky, whose opera *Askold's Grave* kept its place in the repertory for many years. And then there was Dargomïzhsky, an amateur singer and a bold experimenter as a composer. Above all there was Glinka. They belonged to the aristocratic amateur class but they turned themselves into at least semi-professionals and they were all conscious of being Russian. Their social status was a real handicap; even the strongest of them, Glinka, whose two operas are the foundation-stones of classical Russian music, could have achieved very much more if his wealth had not allowed him to indulge his natural indolence and his hypochondria.

Here was a musician with a feeling for the orchestra scarcely inferior to Berlioz's, and who evoked Berlioz's admiration, whose orchestral output apart from his operas amounted to about half-a-dozen quite short pieces, one or two of them (typically) scored for the orchestra of the Governor of Warsaw, where he happened to be staying at the time. He toyed more than once with the idea of symphonies on Russian or Ukrainian themes, only to be checked by the problem of adapting German techniques of thematic development to folk-material to which it was unsuited. A more congenial musical climate might well have braced him to tackle the problem more seriously. The glamour of the opera-house urged him on; the Russian concert-hall as yet had no comparable glamour and offered no comparable opportunity.

It is in this context that we must judge the famous group of nationalist composers who emerged in the second half of the century, the *Kuchka*, the 'little heap' or 'handful' as they were nicknamed. Western writers have often expressed surprise at the fact that composers as considerable as Mussorgsky, Borodin and Rimsky-Korsakov were amateurs with, at the most, a little professional or semi-professional musical training. But there was nothing else they could have been. They were the last and finest products of an eighty-year-old tradition. If a professional musician is one who earns his living by music, he could have done it in early nineteenth-century Russia only by becoming an opera-singer or by giving piano or singing lessons, or some such activity, which a gentleman might indulge in as a hobby but not as a profession. If a professional composer is one who has followed a systematic course of instruction under a master, the position was even more difficult, for there was no conservatoire of music in Russia and no individual master competent to give all-round instruction.

The composers of the *Kuchka* came at the end of the dilettante tradition, though that tradition naturally continued to affect Russian attitudes to music: for instance, the view of chamber music as a relatively lightweight medium has persisted right down to the string quartets of Shostakovich. The dilettante tradition did not die out of its own accord or reform itself from within; it was ended, as it had begun, under the aegis of the Imperial family. At the beginning of the reign of Alexander II when many exhilarating winds of change blew across Russia, Anton Rubinstein, a professional musician if ever there were one, had the ear of the music-loving Grand Duchess Helena Pavlovna, aunt by marriage of the new Tsar. Rubinstein, who was Russian only by birth and commonly regarded by Russians as an outsider, recognized that the country was lagging seriously behind the West so far as higher education in music was concerned. On the initiative of Rubinstein and some of the aristocratic amateurs, and under the patronage and with the financial support of the Grand Duchess, a Russian Musical Society was founded in 1859. The Society brought about two highly important innovations. It established regular series of orchestral concerts: in St. Petersburg almost at once, in Moscow the following year. And, as a result of the Grand Duchess's pressure on the Tsar, it was enabled to set up schools of music: in St. Petersburg in 1862 under Anton Rubinstein himself, in Moscow in 1866 under his brother Nikolay. One of the earliest professors of the Moscow Conservatoire was one of the first graduates of the sister institution in Petersburg: the 26-year-old Chaykovsky, a young man of the same generation and same social background as the *Kuchka* but quite differently conditioned. And of course in 1873 Rimsky-Korsakov, mainly self-educated as he was, joined the staff of the Petersburg Conservatoire and became one of its most distinguished professors. But we should not lose sight of a vital point: the conservatoires and the symphony concerts did not come into existence by a 'natural' process of evolving tradition or as the result of public demand. They came from the energy and enthusiasm and social influence of a small group, the sort of dynamic nucleus which has, time and again in the history of culture, given the lead to the large inert public.

The dilettante tradition did not die without a struggle and a splendid Quixotic attempt to rival the Russian Musical Society in both fields: concert-giving and education. The Grand Duchess Helena Pavlovna was a German by birth and loved German music; so did the doubtfully Russian Rubinstein, who despised Russian amateurism. The original staff of his new Conservatoire consisted in the main of foreigners, and this provoked a vigorous reaction from the Slavophils, the believers in the inherent superiority of everything essentially Russian. The outstanding musical Slavophil was Balakirev, a young man of remarkable gifts and remarkable energy, the former protégé of Ulïbïshev and Glinka, the mentor of Mussorgsky, Rimsky-Korsakov and Borodin. Beginning on the foundation of a friend's amateur choir, Balakirev and some wealthy supporters established in St. Petersburg, also in 1862, a Free School of Music, offering free musical instruction to young people who had neither the money nor the time to study at the Conservatoire. The Free School likewise initiated public orchestral concerts, the programmes of which were largely devoted to the progressive Western composers whom Rubinstein disliked—Schumann, Liszt and Berlioz—and of course to the young Russians. So, thanks to the rivalry of the Russian Music Society and the Free School, St. Petersburg suddenly found itself blessed with two regular series of orchestral concerts, Moscow with one. The consequences in musical creativity showed themselves almost at once. Whereas Russian orchestral music, outside the theatre, had up to now been infinitesimal, it began to pour forth in a stream directly opportunities for performance were offered. Within three decades—say, up to Chaykovsky's death in 1893—practically the entire corpus of what we think of as 'classical Russian orchestral music' was created: the symphonies and other orchestral works of Chaykovsky, Borodin and Rimsky-Korsakov, Balakirev's *Russia* and *Tamara*, the early symphonies of Glazunov.

The younger composers who were able to take advantage of the new opportunities were no longer dilettanti. Of all the dramatic changes that have reorientated the traditions of Russian music so drastically, this was the most fundamental. What was possible within the pure dilettante tradition is demonstrated by the symphonies and songs and string quartets of Borodin, the operas and songs of Mussorgsky. None of the conservatoire-trained composers, except Chaykovsky, had anything like the originality of Borodin, to say nothing of the dramatic genius of Mussorgsky. But the man who has been taught the craft of composition and commands all its devices and rules-of-thumb has enormous advantages over the amateur, particularly in the construction of large-scale works like opera and, even more, symphonies. Where the amateur has to plod, working out everything painfully, the professional rides swiftly and easily on the wheels of technique. One need only study Mussorgsky's struggles with his operas or read Rimsky-Korsakov's own account of his fumblings with his First Symphony and his first opera, to see the difficulties that beset even the most gifted dilettante. But facility easily becomes fatal. Technical facility not only enabled Chaykovsky and the later Rimsky-Korsakov to turn out great quantities of music in which inspiration runs rather thin; it encouraged a great outpouring of beautifully made, euphonious music which sounds no greater depths and scales not many greater heights than the dilettante music of the earlier part of the century. Only it is much **more** skilfully made and much greater in quantity.

*　　*　　*

Not all the blame for this is to be laid to the account of technical facility. The political and cultural ambience again played its part. I have mentioned the many bracing winds that swept Russia in the early 1860s. It was a period of high hopes under a relatively liberal-minded Emperor, hopes that were fulfilled so far as the emancipation of the serfs was concerned. The world of literature and art was dominated by the thinking of Belinsky and Chernïshevsky, who demanded that the arts should be related to life and true to life, not academic or devoted to beauty for its own sake. This was the aesthetic basis of Mussorgsky's thought and in various ways it underlay the novels of Tolstoy and Dostoevsky, the plays of Ostrovsky and the paintings of Repin. But the vision faded and, when in March 1881 Alexander II was assassinated and Mussorgsky died a drunkard's death in a military hospital a fortnight later, neither had fulfilled the hopes once placed in him and neither had remained quite true to his principles. From then until the Revolution Russia lay under a cloud of political reaction beneath which free thought would have been completely crushed if Tolstoy's courage and prestige had not given him a position in which he could defy Orthodoxy and autocracy almost single-handed—except when the working-classes boiled up in the proto-revolution of 1905. Poets took refuge in Parnassianism and symbolism, thinkers in mysticism and esoteric religious cults, artists escaped from reality into art-for-art's-sake. This was the society whose spirit was distilled by Chekhov, who gently laughed at it and immortally preserved it. It is not surprising that in this environment Russian music turned to the expression of elegant, elegiac sentimentality or escaped into fairy-tale worlds or simply to music-for-music's-sake. Both the sentimentality and the love of fairy-tales had played a part in the Russian musical tradition from the time it really began in the eighteenth century. But now they filled the entire scene. By a strange chance, this period when the highest wave of Russian music had expended its force, the quarter of a century before the Revolution, was the period in which it made its strongest impact on the rest of the Western world, its real contribution to the European main stream.

I shall return, in another context, to the impact of the Russian

Revolution and the consequences of Soviet policy towards music. But this sketchy account of the peculiar zigzag course of Russia's musical tradition may help to show how much that occurred after 1917 was not exactly latent in what had gone before, though some of it was, but might be expected in Russia much more than in any other country. Church music—and consequently Russian music as a sophisticated art generally—suffered crippling limitation for centuries through a religious decision. Russian music was very belatedly brought into contact with that of Europe as a result of political action (Peter I's policy of Westernization) and his niece's importation of Italian opera; it was set on yet another new course in the middle of the nineteenth century when Court intervention suddenly steered it away from aristocratic dilettantism to European-style professionalism. Russian musical tradition was well accustomed to being taken vigorously in hand by authority long before the Central Committee of the All-Union Communist Party seized it by the scruff of the neck in April 1932 and gave it, with the other Soviet arts, the slogan of 'Socialist realism.' And we must bear in mind that many of the ideas of Socialist realism were implicit, even explicit, in Chernïshevsky's *Aesthetic Relations of Art and Reality* in the middle of the nineteenth century and Tolstoy's *What is Art?* at its end; we attribute to Communism much that is really Russian. The policy adopted in 1932 and broadly maintained since then, though it has sometimes been relaxed and sometimes tightened again, was essentially an official attempt to freeze tradition, just as the Orthodox Church managed to freeze the tradition of its music for so many centuries. And since Communism may be regarded as a species of secular religion—which plays much the same role in the propagation of modern Russian imperialism that Catholicism played in the propagation of Spanish imperialism and Protestantism in that of Anglo-Saxon imperialism—the parallel is quite close.

The musical tradition that 'Socialist realism' has attempted to maintain in a frozen state was a thoroughly Russian tradition. (This applies to Russia proper, of course; the Caucasian and Asiatic republics of the Soviet Union have been encouraged to develop their own folk-traditions.) The ideal models have been the classic masters of the nineteenth century from Glinka to Chaykovsky and Rimsky-Korsakov. Their idiom could be harmonically spiced to some extent but not to an extent that utterly distorted it. There must be no playing with the foreign techniques of Schoenberg and other 'modernists' of the outside world: this was 'formalism', music-for-music's-sake, without 'social content'. And, for good or ill, the policy by and large succeeded in its purpose for a long time. Tradition was not completely frozen but it was enormously and unnaturally slowed down.

The irony of the present situation is that a musical policy which attached so much importance to social relevance appears to be in process of erosion by precisely that: social relevance. Soviet music could be guarded successfully against the Central European innovators who were over-sophisticating the traditional language of music. Such innovations were primarily a professional affair, for musicians only, and secondarily for a small, highly cultivated sector of the general public. But the Soviet Union is itself a society undergoing vast and rapid changes; it is now very different from the society of the early 1930s which was content with Socialist realism in the form of extreme conservatism. A largely technological, scientifically minded society is being reflected in, and interested by, a music much more radical than Schoenberg's. As recently as 1957 Andrey Volkonsky's dodecaphonic piano suite *Musica stricta* could be brushed aside as 'nothing more than a fashionable experiment' and the composition of genuinely contemporary music was a more or less underground activity. But Nono, Stockhausen and Boulez have achieved a breakthrough in the Soviet Union much more effective than that of the pre-war and immediate post-war modernists. Aleatoric and electronic techniques are being employed, not exactly with the blessing of the leaders of the Union of Soviet Composers but no longer clandestinely. Such music is publicly performed by well-known artists—for instance, under a conductor as distinguished as Rozhdestvensky—and seriously discussed, not merely abused, at meetings of the Union of Soviet Composers and in its official organ, *Sovetskaya Muzïka*.

'And how,' it may be asked, 'does this music stand in relation to the specifically Russian tradition?' The answer appears to be, 'Nowhere.' Just as technological man becomes more and more international, our cities get more and more alike and one cosmonaut is pretty much like another, the most advanced music usually appears to have no national characteristics. I say 'appears' because we are too close to it to hear it in perspective. Future historians may indeed detect traces of national tradition in the aleatoric music of the 1960s in France or Germany or Russia. We cannot.

IV

THE FACTOR OF LANGUAGE

Nationality has long been recognized as both a formative and a divisive factor in musical tradition. But 'nationality' is a loose and unsatisfactory term. It leads into an area of facile generalizations and even if we recognize the deep differences in temperament and outlook between French and Germans, between Scots and Italians, directly we try to formulate them methodically we run into innumerable difficulties and find innumerable exceptions, and we may end by wondering whether there was all that difference in temperament between Giuseppe Verdi and Thomas Carlyle. So far as music is concerned, the only clear-cut criterion of nationality is language.

We have already seen how the mere fitting of German words to plainsong could produce a subtle change of musical character, even before the different language began to work on it more deeply. Not merely different vowels and consonants are substituted, but different qualities of vowels and consonants. (This is one of the numerous problems of foreign opera in English; it is not that English is a bad language for singing—it is actually better than some—but it is less good than Italian or French for singing Italian or French music.) The nature of a people's language inevitably affects the nature of its music not only in obvious and superficial ways but fundamentally. It is not merely that a language rich in feminine endings, as Italian is, will generate a great number of musical phrases with feminine endings and incite composers to devise new ways of treating them, such as Puccini's repetition of the last stressed note for the unstressed syllable instead of a falling cadence. Or that languages such as Hungarian and Czech, in which the first syllable of each word is invariably stressed, are unlikely to generate melodies beginning with upbeats. A language like Italian, rich in broad open vowels on which the voice can rest and unfold its tone, a language rich in liquid consonants which give no more than a slight edge to the vowels without clogging them, and in which the grammatical usage (except in some dialects perhaps) is to make every construction as liquescent as possible—such a language could hardly fail to produce a tradition of song. The tradition of song—rich, full, penetrating but not marked by outstanding rhythmic vitality—is the basis of Italian music in general. Naturally it has not been the sole formative factor; but it has been the strongest factor. And this inherent vocality has had far-reaching consequences.

While almost all European musics were no doubt vocal in origin, with a 'high culture' main stream stemming from plainsong, Italian music has preserved that quality more effortlessly and cultivated it more richly than any other, not only in music actually sung but in instrumental music. It is significant that by far the most important instrument evolved by the Italian genius has been the violin, an instrument which with its vibrato manner of performance (in distinction from the older viol family) emulates and even surpasses the human voice. The practice of any instrument naturally leads to the exploration and exploitation of all its capabilities; it was discovered that the violin could do many other things besides sing. But it was left for a German, Johann Sebastian Bach, to experiment with the solo violin in what is essentially a keyboard style, exploiting its capacity for polyphony with a brilliant perversity that is equalled only by Italian perversity in making the human voice emulate the agility and even idiom of the violin. In contrast to Bach, whatever Corelli demanded of the violin was violinistic; the outstanding quality of his music is its golden, singing melody, comparable with the actually vocal cantabile of Alessandro Scarlatti. Corelli's violin cantabile may have no vowels, but the vowels are immanent.

It is true that quasi-vocal melody is not the outstanding characteristic of Scarlatti's son, Domenico. But Domenico's instrument was the harpsichord, an instrument incapable of cantabile, and most of the works by which we know him were composed in Spain, many of them under the evident influence of the guitar sound. When an Italian, Bartolomeo Cristofori, invented the *gravecembalo con piano e forte*, the first pianoforte, an instrument capable of more sustained tone than the harpsichord, it was Italianate Germans—Johann Christian Bach and Mozart—and a native Italian, Clementi, who exploited the instrument's pseudo-cantabile rather than its dynamic potential while Johann Christian's brother, Carl Philipp Emanuel, a true North German by environment and temperament, when he wanted to give the instrument something like a human voice, wrote for it not quasi-cantabile but quasi-recitative. After J. C. Bach and Mozart, a Clementi pupil, John Field, and a Pole deeply imbued with the idiom of Italian opera, Chopin, between them developed a piano-style that does not merely disguise by ornamentation the instrument's inability to sustain sound at the same level but makes a virtue of necessity and treats the dying sound in such a way as to produce an illusion of cantabile.

The most important musical form Italy has given us is, of course, opera. In its origin opera was an intellectual conception: the idea of a music entirely subordinated to the text, a music simply for reciting the words in natural speech-rhythm and with appropriately rising and falling pitch—recitative. The earliest operas, the operas of Peri and Caccini and Marco da Gagliano, are not much more than that: dramas in recitative. And if opera had remained not much more than that, it would have remained an interesting historical curiosity but would never have become one of the great art forms of Western civilization. The fact that it did not is solely attributable to one thing—the breaking through of the irrepressible Italian instinct for song, even in Peri's *Euridice* in the nymph's strophic song and Orfeo's 'Gioite al canto mio' in the last scene:

Ex. 11

64

- se. Gio - i - te a-ma - ti col - li e d'o - gni in-tor - no

Less than a decade after Peri, Monteverdi wrote his *Orfeo*, the earliest opera which is not merely a historical curiosity, and it is by no means a pure drama in recitative. However Monteverdi tried, like Boswell's friend, to be philosophical, cheerfulness in the form of frank melody kept powerfully breaking in—madrigalian choruses much more extended than, say, Peri's 'Ben nocchier costante'; instrumental pieces more numerous and more significant than Peri's little ritornelli; and, above all, great solo songs like Orfeo's 'Qual onor':

Ex. 12

Qual o - nor____ di te sia de - gno mia cet - ra on-ni - po-ten-te,

s'hai nel Tar-ta - reo reg - no pie-gar po - tu - to o-gni in-du - ra - ta men - te.

The damage to the purely intellectual conception was fortunately irreparable. Recitative remained for a time the main musical element in opera and continued to remain so *in theory* much longer; but it was not sensitively composed recitative that sent crowds flocking to the many opera houses that opened to the Venetian and other Italian publics during the course of the century. It was—next to the scenic wonders—the interpolated arias. In little more than half a century the intellectual conception of opera lay in ruins. With Marc' Antonio Cesti and Stradella recitative became ever more perfunctory, the arias more and more numerous. In his *Floridoro* Stradella gave his public thirty-seven arias accompanied by continuo only and sixteen more with *obbligato* violin parts. The way was open to the golden age of the *da capo* aria, with Alessandro Scarlatti and that very Italianized German, Handel. From time to time various foreigners tried to restore the supremacy of drama over music. Lully tried—an Italian by birth, it is true, but taken to France at a very early age and brought up as a musician in a purely French environment. Then Gluck tried, and Wagner tried. But we never hear of an Italian pioneer of opera reform; Boito, Verdi in his old age, and Puccini in the 1890s were only responding to the spirit of their age.

For the other side of the coin we must look at what happened to Italian instrumental music from the time of Beethoven onward. So long as instrumental melody remained still within arm's length of vocal melody, Italian instrumental music continued to be nourished by its true source. But the nineteenth century brought in more specifically instrumental types of melody, and composers struggled constantly, though not always successfully, to follow Beethoven in *motivische Arbeit*, thematic work with smaller melodic units instead of the long-drawn songlike type. So during the century of Rossini, Bellini, Donizetti, Verdi, Catalani, and Puccini with their wonderful long-breathed tunes, Italian orchestral music existed mainly in the form of a few largely perfunctory opera overtures, while the chamber music amounts to nothing more than Verdi's single quartet and some pleasant curiosities by Rossini and Donizetti. It is true that towards the end of the century Sgambati and Martucci did their best to bring about a renaissance of instrumental music, but how many of their compositions are ever heard today? Even the famous 'generation of '80'—Pizzetti, Malipiero, and Casella—working in a different intellectual climate, have been most successful with vocal music or fairly melodious instrumental music. And can we not say the same of

Dallapiccola? Even in *avant-garde* Italian music a sensitive listener can still perceive the element of immanent cantilena. Only the other day a colleague told me he had observed to Luciano Berio that he was a master of *bel canto*; Berio was taken aback, but I think my friend had made a penetrating observation.

* * *

I want now to turn to the other extreme, from a music based on open, expansive vowel sounds to one generated by a language rather poor in them and also marked by some awkward compound consonants. No doubt, a philologist could tell us why Czech is poorer in this respect than the other Slavonic languages, but the fact is certainly not connected with any deficiency of musicality for, as everyone knows, the Czechs abound in it. Charles Burney tells us that in his day they had the reputation of being 'the most musical people of Germany, or perhaps of all Europe'[1] and J. F. Reichardt says pretty much the same in his *Briefe eines aufmerksamen Reisenden*. But a language in which some vowels are rather pinched and a number of monosyllables and stressed syllables have no true vowel at all—e.g. *Vl*tava, *Br*no, *sr*pen (August), *prst* (finger), *trh* (market)— will not, of course, prevent people from singing but it is unlikely to encourage a great tradition of song or of music based on song. The most characteristic Czech folk-songs are dance-songs, consequently with short note-values, strongly marked metres, and short phrases; even the slow songs are not particularly long-breathed. A great quantity of Czech song has come down to us from the Hussite time, the early fifteenth century—religious and warlike songs preserved in the Hussite song-books—but they are not expansive songs. They are mainly syllabic; the tune exists primarily to carry the words. 'Ye warriors of God' is the most famous of them all and the only one generally known to us, because Smetana used it in two numbers of *Má Vlast*, and Dvořák in his *Hussite Overture*, and Janáček in his opera *Mr. Brouček*; it is typical in its repeated notes, its relatively small compass and its rhythmic emphasis:[2]

[1] *The Present State of Music in Germany* (London, 1773), II, pp. 3 ff.
[2] Earliest version, from the *Jistebnický Kancionál* (*c.* 1420).

Ex. 13

Ktož jsú bo - ží   bo - jo -vni - ci   a zá - ko - na je - ho.

Here we have the absolute antithesis of Italian song. Whoever composed that melody attached little importance to tone for its own sake; the music was first and last a vehicle for the words. Whereas beautiful Italian song is carried on the wings of the language, beautiful Czech song is a triumph over the language.

The same might be said of Hungarian peasant-song. Philologically the Hungarian language is as remote from Czech as it is from most other European tongues but it does have in common with it something more than that invariable tonic accent on the first syllable; it has some rather awkward vowels. It is not, I am sure, a matter of chance that so many of that vast collection of Hungarian peasant-songs amassed by Bartók and Kodály and their successors are tunes of small compass with small rise and fall and short note-values. They are in fact melodized speech. And this quality naturally penetrated deeply into the music of the master who studied them so lovingly. Consider the third of Bartók's *Improvisations on Hungarian Peasant Songs* for piano:

Ex. 14

Lento, rubato

68

This is a long way from a '*song* without words'; Bartók significantly marks it *quasi parlando*, not *cantabile*. And this *parlando* quality is perceptible in a great many of his original instrumental themes; they are 'music without words' yet they seem to imply words. His only opera, *Duke Bluebeard's Castle*, is a *locus classicus* of the application of the Hungarian folk-idiom (not actual folk-melody) in sophisticated music; it consists of so many repeated notes or small intervals in speech-rhythm that even Kodály at first took it for recitative. This is equally true of his best solo songs, the Ady settings, Op. 16. To say that Bartók's melodic lines are not always like this is only to say that folk-music was not the only formative element in his style.

This attitude to song, conditioned by language, shows itself in various ways in the sophisticated music of both the Czechs and the Hungarians. (I say 'sophisticated music' advisedly, for to speak of it as 'art-music' or 'composed music' seems to imply that folk-music was either not composed or not art.) The attitude is most strikingly evident in the relative neglect of solo song by Czech and Hungarian composers. They do not neglect it altogether; few composers can completely resist the temptation to set the poems of their own language; but solo song never plays an important part, either quantitatively or qualitatively, in their output. Nor does singing in Czech music-making. I have already quoted Burney on the Czechs' reputation for musicality. He also had his views on the formation of traditions of musicality:

I never could suppose effects without a cause [he says]; nature, though often partial to individuals, in her distribution of genius and talents, is never so to a whole people. Climate contributes greatly to the forming of customs and manners; and it is, I believe, certain that those who inhabit hot climates are more delighted with music than those of cold ones; perhaps, from the auditory nerves being more irritable in the one than in the other, and from sound being propagated with greater facility: but I could, by no means, account for climate operating more in favour of music upon the Bohemians, than on their neighbours, the Saxons and Moravians.

Of course, Burney was in a muddle, for in common usage the term Czechs, or 'Bohemians' as Burney calls them, includes the Moravians (though not the Slovaks) and the Moravians are at least as musical as the Czechs proper. (As for the Saxons, they had already produced Schütz, Bach and Handel, and were going to produce Schumann and Wagner among others.) Burney 'crossed the whole kingdom of Bohemia, from south to north', he tells us, and was 'very assiduous' in 'enquiries how the common people learned music'. He found it was universally taught in the village schools. But to me the most significant thing about his first-hand account is what it does not report. At one place, Čáslav near Kolín, he found the school

> full of little children of both sexes, from six to ten or eleven years old, who were reading, writing, playing on violins, hautbois, bassoons, and other instruments. The organist had in a small room of his house four clavichords, with little boys practising on them all.

Later this organist, who was one of the two schoolmasters, the other being a violinist, improvised a fugue 'in a very masterly manner'. In Prague

> an itinerant band of street-musicians came to salute me at the inn ... during dinner; they played upon the harp, violin, and horn, several minuets and Polonoises.

He enumerates various eminent violinists and other instrumentalists and comments that 'the Bohemians are remarkably expert in the use of wind instruments in general'. At Budin he

> found a music school; and heard two of the poor boys perform in the street, one on the harp, and the other on the triangles, tolerably well.

All these passages refer exclusively to instrumental performance; there is not a word about singing, even choral singing. At Lobeschütz, it is true, he visited the church and mentions that 'here the children vocally and instrumentally perform', going on to add that

I heard a considerable number of the boys practising on the fiddle, at school, but in a very coarse manner.

The only real reference to singing in the whole of Burney's account of his travels in Bohemia concerns Prague, where Josef Seger

informed me, that at the convent of the Holy Cross, where he is organist, there are now three or four boys, brought thither from country schools, who sing most admirably; having good voices, and good shakes, with good taste and expression.

All this intensive cultivation of instrumental performance, and only three or four boys—whom Burney seems not to have actually heard—who were said to sing well!

The record of history amply supports Burney's observations. The Czechs excel in instrumental music, and just as Italian instrumental music is permeated by cantabile, so Czech vocal music is apt to be instrumental in essence. In opera, the vocal medium in which the Czechs have most distinguished themselves, this is particularly noticeable. Dvořák is the most melodious of Czech opera-composers, but his melodies are at least as instrumental as they are vocal; they certainly do not arise out of the nature of the human voice. And this is even more true of the majority of Smetana's operas. Song predominates in *The Bartered Bride*, without the tunes being particularly vocal, and in his other operas the voice tends to rest on the surface of a rather Lisztian orchestral texture. Janáček is even more significant, for he made an almost lifelong study of speech-inflexions. When a musician is particularly sensitive to speech-inflexion, the normal consequence is that he stylizes words and phrases by little musical exaggerations. But Janáček delighted in 'photographing' speech, in pinning it down in musical notation with the greatest possible precision. Instead of a singing melody, the result is an angular motive in short note-values, which he was quite willing to use in the vocal line of an opera but which he never fails to employ as an instrumental motive. Nor can I believe it is by chance that the Czechs, from Benda in the eighteenth century to Fibich in the late nineteenth, are the only musicians who have attempted *full-length* melodrama: not merely passages of spoken dialogue accompanied or interspersed with music but opera-length spoken dramas with orchestral accompaniment.

One of Beethoven's Czech contemporaries, Tomášek, actually prefaced a song-cycle to Czech words with a defence of his native language as suitable for musical treatment, but he composed far more German songs than Czech ones. (But that, admittedly, may have been for commercial reasons; Bohemia had a large German-speaking population until after 1918.) But his songs, German and Czech alike, are forgotten while his piano music is recognized as at least historically important. His brilliant young contemporary Jan Václav Voříšek, whose instrumental music has deservedly survived and is still performed and recorded for the gramophone, set only German texts to music. It is the same with the better known Czech composers of later times. Except for a few juvenilia, Smetana's only solo songs are the cycle of *Večerní písně* (Evening Songs), and these are either declamatory or pianistic, the piano-part obviously conceived first and the words fitted to it. Dvořák was a more prolific song-composer but it is significant that when in later life he turned to his early, mainly unpublished cycle *Cypresses*, he revised only eight of them as songs, the ones we know as Op. 83, and preferred to recast twelve as pieces for string quartet. Like Tomášek, he often set German words; probably his best-known cycle, the *Gypsy Songs*, was originally composed to German verses. The *Biblical Songs*, largely declamatory, were set to Czech words and Dvořák made considerable modifications in the voice-part for the German edition, which gives us a chance to compare his reactions to the two languages. Take, for instance, the opening of 'The Lord is my shepherd', Op. 99, no. 4:

Ex. 15 *(a)*

72

Equally significant in a different way is the nature of the inspiration Dvořák drew from a favourite collection of poems, the *Kytice* (Bouquet) of Karel Jaromír Erben, a book of lyrical poems embodying popular fancies or related to folk-customs, and narrative ballads based on folk-tales. Dvořák turned to Erben's poems a number of times, yet only twice for *vocal* music: for a song, 'The Orphan', Op. 5, and for the text of the choral work known in Britain and America as *The Spectre's Bride*. But the *Kytice* gave him the ideas—not merely the programmes but the musical themes—of at least four, and almost certainly more, instrumental compositions. The four which are avowedly based on Erben's poems are the symphonic poems *The Water-Sprite*, *The Noonday Witch*, *The Golden Spinning-Wheel* and *The Wood-Dove*. Dvořák's composition-sketches[3] show that at least in *The Water-Sprite*, *The Golden Spinning-Wheel* and *The Wood-Dove* he began by pencilling down a melodic line directly suggested by the words, which he sometimes actually wrote underneath. In *The Water-Sprite* he started with the fifth stanza and went steadily on through the eighth, though he did not bother to go on writing in the text. This melodic line was the raw material from which he went on to extract a tiny motive here or a more extended theme there to be polished up into its final form. In *The Wood-Dove* he wrote out the words of the first three stanzas under his melodic line, and reached the third stanza before the words gave him anything usable. At the beginning of *The Golden Spinning-Wheel* he did not take the trouble to write in the words at all, yet the music fits them very closely even in the definitive score.

Ex. 16

Naturally these verbally inspired themes and passages are not confined to the openings of the poems; here and there a significant

---

[3] Partly published in facsimile in Antonín Sychra, *Estetika Dvořákovy symfonické tvorby* (Prague, 1959), following p. 520. Sychra discusses the sketches in detail, pp. 43–54 and 114–30.

line gives him a motive to be used as it stands, or more often to be improved, as symphonic material. This habit of slightly remoulding the verbally inspired ideas makes it difficult to trace them elsewhere, especially as we lack the clues of titles and avowed programmes. But I have found that at least two of the *Legends*, Op. 59, can be similarly related to poems in Erben's *Kytice*. For instance, the opening theme of the very first of the *Legends* fits almost exactly the first line of a poem entitled 'The Daughter's Curse' ('Why look so sad and gloomy, daughter mine?'):

Ex. 17

The poem is a mother-and-daughter dialogue exactly on the lines of the mother-son dialogue in the Scottish ballad of 'Edward' which Erben no doubt knew in Herder's German translation, and Dvořák's music corresponds perfectly. Again, there is a poem sometimes printed as supplement to the *Kytice* which commemorates the Battle of Domažlice, one of the greatest of all the Hussite victories, written in couplets which exactly fit the principal theme of the fourth *Legend*:

Ex. 18

This is very like the Hussite songs and the whole piece can easily be heard as a Hussite war-song, brief battle, and triumph. Thus the words of probably half-a-dozen, certainly four poems from this one collection—possibly even more—inspired Dvořák to instrumental compositions as against two vocal settings.

Other composers have found inspiration for instrumental themes in verbal phrases—Brahms, for instance—but, so far as I know, none has done so to the same extent as Dvořák—except Janáček. Janáček's acute ear for the musical inflexions of everyday speech provided him with a whole storehouse of instrumental ideas. To take a well authenticated example: at the opening of his wind sextet, *Mládí* (Youth) the oboe utters a theme based on the exclamation, 'Mládí. Zlaté mládí'—'Youth. Golden youth':

Ex. 19

Often in his operas Janáček will pick up some vocal intonation, not necessarily a very striking one, pass it to the orchestra and employ it quasi-symphonically for a while, though not as a *Leitmotiv*, and not specially associated with the words that generated it. He does the same thing in his song-cycle *The Diary of One Who Vanished*, which is his sole important contribution to Czech solo song. (Even that is semi-dramatic in that the protagonist is a dramatic character, that another soloist and three voices perhaps representing the voice of the forest are actually heard in three numbers, and that Janáček wished the work to be performed on a partly darkened stage with a hint of action.) His ear for the musical inflexions of speech did not make him a song-composer. Yet he wrote choral music, not only the great *Glagolitic Mass* but shorter choral pieces of considerable power. So, for that matter, did Dvořák and Smetana. I will not labour the points that the best of it is dramatic in essence and that much of Dvořák's is set to Latin texts. The existence of some sort of choral tradition has always been guaranteed by the Church, and the Roman Church has happily provided the musicians of all Catholic countries with an alternative language, eminently singable, whatever the vernacular may be.

Like the impact of the intellectual conceptions of the Renaissance on Italian music—word-painting in the madrigal, subordination of music to text in early opera—the influence of a choral tradition on Czech music is a characteristic example of the dilution of tradition. But dilution implies a weakening, whereas these impacts and influences are often enrichments. The formatives of any kind of musical tradition are diverse and numerous, and even in this single area of language it would not be easy to find in Western culture other such relatively clear-cut examples of musics so largely conditioned by the nature of languages as Italian and Czech, though an ethnomusicologist would probably have no difficulty in producing plenty from the non-Western cultures which have been less subject to cross-influences of every kind. Very few Western musics have stopped their ears to the siren sounds of Italian music. The singing Italian style was emulated by the early sixteenth-century Franco-Flemings who conquered Italy and were conquered by it, by the English madrigalists, and by the opera-composers of every age and nation, including some of those, like Weber and Wagner, who resisted it most self-consciously. When a Czech composer, František Václav Míča, who flourished in the 1730s, wrote an opera on a national subject, *L'origine di Jaromeritz in Moravia*, he wrote it not only to an Italian libretto but in what one can only call Italian music, and the music was left unchanged when he afterwards had a Czech version fitted to it (which must have presented the singers with some problems). Yet underneath this Italian accent acquired by Czech and French and German and English composers one can recognize without too much difficulty their native musical speech, shaped by the spoken language, though seldom as obviously as in the two extreme cases we have been considering.

* * *

Assimilation is naturally easiest in those areas where the languages are closest, not philologically but in musical characteristics. Thus Russian, with its wealth of musical vowels and consonants can assimilate Italian musical influences very easily, and has sometimes done so with fatal ease when it has not been consciously resisted. But there is no need to look for Italian influence behind Russian lyricism, the main source of which lies in the language itself. Mussorgsky was as little touched by Italian influence as any musician has been, and there is a vast proportion of lyrical, eminently vocal music in his work as a whole. And this is not to be attributed solely to folk-music as its source. As one would expect with a language so rich in open vowels, Russian folk-song is quite exceptionally rich in long-sustained sounds; one of the recognized varieties of Russian folk-song is the *protryazhnaya pesn*, the 'protracted song'. But although Mussorgsky's melody is often marked by the modes and intonations of folk-music and sometimes approximates to it very closely, as in the opening bars of *Boris Godunov*, a great deal of it is not. Neither Boris's monologue, 'I stand supreme in power', nor his death scene has any demonstrable connection with folk-music. It is difficult to think of any Russian composer of any note, even the most 'instrumental' ones such as Rimsky-Korsakov and Skryabin, who has not had at his command a fund of lyrical, vocal or quasi-vocal, melody. But the case of Mussorgsky is particularly interesting on account of his aim at deliberate naturalism, his attention to the inflexions of speech, comparable with Janáček's yet so different. He did attempt an opera based entirely on speech-intonations, a setting of Gogol's prose comedy *Marriage*, but abandoned it after one act; in his mature operas melody kept breaking in, in *Boris* as it had done in Monteverdi's *Orfeo*, and in *Khovanshchina* it swamped everything. In one of the most naturalistic of his songs, 'Savishna', the village idiot pleading with the village beauty, the poor boy's speech is certainly not as melodious as the lament of that other idiot in *Boris* but it is by no means recitative. It is stylized in short, continuous, repeated melodic phrases:

Ex. 20
Fairly fast

Svet moy Sa - vish - na, so - kol yas - nen - ky. Po - lyu - bi me - nya ne ra - zum - no - va,

Most European languages occupy the middle ground between those poor in vowels, like Hungarian and Czech, and the rich ones like Italian and Russian. English, German and Spanish all belong in different ways to this class. Naturally a number of other linguistic factors play a formative role in music. The various peculiarities of French have combined to give French vocal music a particularly close relationship with words. The advantages of German vowels are partially offset by the clogging effect of German consonants and perhaps these consonants are the reason for the sober pulse of so much German vocal, and hence instrumental, music. The music of Bach and Beethoven, Schumann and Brahms, Wagner and Bruckner, whatever it is, is not light-footed. As we have seen, the simple substitution of a German text for a Latin one deprives plainsong of something of its flow and elasticity, and the continuous tendency— what one might call the compounding of tradition—in the hands of such composers as Schein and Bach was to make the melody still more even and square-cut; they imposed on it more rhythmic sobriety instead of injecting rhythmic vitality. The ponderously metrical rhyming verses create squarely balanced melodic phrases. At their most typical, the Lutheran hymn melodies are in common time, even when, as in the case of 'Wie schön' leuchtet der Morgenstern', they have passed through a phase of scansion in triple time. And while no one is going to be so absurd as to deny that a quantity of great and characteristic German music has been written in triple time, metrical squareness and the sturdy march of common time do seem to be highly characteristic features of German music. No one was more agonizingly conscious of this than the mature Wagner after he found he had composed *Lohengrin* entirely in common time, but for one short passage. Again and again after that, we find him painstakingly rewriting in triple time music he had originally conceived in 4/4: the song of the sirens and Venus's 'Geliebter, komm!' in the original *Tannhäuser*, recast in the Paris version;[4] the last strophe of the Prize Song as it appears in the *Meistersinger* overture, recast when it appears in the opera—the overture was written first; and the melody to which Brünnhilde sings 'O Siegfried, Herrlicher! Hort der Welt!' in Act III of *Siegfried* which was rewritten in 3/4 a year or so later in the *Siegfried Idyll*.

I suggest that this tendency of German music is mainly, if not solely, attributable to German prosody. The fact that German verse is based on stress does not mark it as different from most modern languages. But the earliest rhythmical organization of European

---

[4] See my *Slavonic and Romantic Music* (London, 1968), pp. 304-5.

music was not suggested by the vernacular languages; it was based on Latin prosody which was, of course, quantitative. The commonest pattern of quantitative verse is the simple alternation of long and short syllables; consequently the commonest rhythmic pattern of Western European music in the earliest period of rhythmic notation was basically an alternation of long and short notes, as in the first two of the so-called 'rhythmic modes' (but centuries before this theory of rhythmic modes was evolved), each long note having the value of two short ones. Such a basic alternation of long and short notes naturally produces triple time and it is not, I hope, too fanciful to see in this circumstance the origin of the innumerable English, French and Italian dances and old popular songs in 6/8 time. But the German-speaking lands were late-comers to the European concert. Specifically German music, at any rate in its surviving forms, was shaped by German verse uninhibited by a strong heritage of modal rhythm and marked by the alternation of heavy and light syllables instead of long and short ones. (Early German poetry had two stressed syllables in each verse.) And whereas the alternation of long and short notes tends to produce triple time, the alternation of stressed and unstressed ones tends to produce common time. It *can* also be translated into triple time, but (to take one body of examples) it has always seemed to me that the *Minnesänger* contrafacta of *trouvère* songs sound more convincing when transmuted from modal rhythm to common time and I diffidently suggest that modal rhythm has been applied to them too often in modern transcriptions.

* * *

Through the greater part of the Middle Ages England was not only close to the musical centre of Europe but shared its language. Norman-French was the cultural language until the thirteenth century and by the time English, which itself had at one time had quantitative vowels and which by now had been infiltrated more and more by Norman-French, took its place as the literary language, English musicians had already acquired a tradition of modal scansion in setting secular texts. Thus the settings of Middle English poems such as 'Mirie it is' and 'Worldes bliss', the melodies of which

79

are in non-mensural notation, seem to demand transcription in
triple time:

Similarly, while the original notation of 'Sumer is icumen in' appears
to be non-mensural it is difficult to accept anything but trochaic
scansion—musically, triple time—and the later scribe who brought
the notation up to date obviously had no doubts. Yet, owing to the
hybrid nature of our language, ambiguities remain and the result of
this hybridism has perhaps been to deprive the language of any
obvious, positive formative influence on English or American music,
though it offers musicians a rich variety of phonetic raw material.

How different the position is with French! The musical properties
of no other language have been so often, and so bitterly, discussed.
The Abbé Raguenet was perhaps the first to put the cat among the
pigeons when he published his *Parallèle des Italiens et des Français
en ce qui regarde la musique et les opéras* in 1702. I quote from the
anonymous English translation of 1709.[5] The Italian language, he
says,

> is much more naturally adapted to music than ours; their vowels
> are all sonorous, whereas above half of ours are mute or at best
> bear a very small part in pronunciation, so that, in the first place,
> no cadence or beautiful passage can be formed upon the syllables
> that consist of those vowels, and, in the next, the words are
> expressed by halves, so that we are left to guess at what the French
> are singing, whereas the Italian is perfectly understood. Besides,

[5] Reprinted by Oliver Strunk, *Source Readings in Music History* (New York, 1950),
p. 476.

though all the Italian vowels are full and open, yet the composers choose out of them such as they judge most proper for their finest divisions. They generally make choice of the vowel *a*, which, being clearer and more distinct than any of the rest, expresses the beauty of the cadence and division to a better advantage. Whereas we make use of all the vowels indifferently, those that are mute as well as those that are sonorous; nay, very often we pitch upon a diphthong, as in the words *chaîne* and *gloire*, which syllables, consisting of two vowels joined together, create a confused sound and want that clearness and beauty that we find in the simple vowels.

Rousseau said many similar and still more unkind things half a century later in his *Lettre sur la musique française*, winding up with the sweeping assertion that 'there is neither measure nor melody in French music, because the language is not capable of them'.[6] Admittedly those French forward vowels present difficulties; if Russian is 'the Italian of the Slav languages' as someone has said, French might be called 'the Czech of the Latin languages'. But it is fatuous to compare French with Italian in this way and assert that vowel-poverty leads to worse music. It does not; it leads to a different music. When Rousseau stops talking about the *a priori* superiority of Italian music and the general badness of mid-eighteenth-century French recitative, and makes a positive observation, he goes straight to the mark:

It is evident on all grounds that the recitative most suitable to the French language must be almost the opposite of that which is in use; that it must range within very small intervals, without much raising or lowering of the voice; with few prolonged notes, no sudden outbursts, still fewer shrieks; especially nothing which resembles melody; little inequality in the duration or value of the notes or in their intensity either.[7]

One might imagine he was describing the voice-parts of *Pelléas et Mélisande*. But it was not left to Debussy to discover that Rousseau

[6] ibid., p. 654.   [7] ibid., p. 652.

was right. This was instinctively understood by the most French of French composers, those who were least distracted by Italian or German models. French vocal music has for a very long time tended to stand in a peculiarly close relationship to the words, to the text itself—not merely to the emotion expressed by the text. I think of the sixteenth-century *musique mesurée* of the time of the *Pléiade*, a music entirely controlled by the scansion of the verse, of Lully's recitative which (however Rousseau may have disliked the tradition it started) was based on the declamation of the greatest French tragic actress of his day, Racine's pupil and mistress, La Champmeslé, the vocal writing of Berlioz's operas, the later songs of Fauré such as those of *La bonne chanson*. The Italian language is so musical in itself that it seems to generate an autonomous music, music that could lose the words without much harm; French generates music that is inseparable from itself. The long-breathed melodic line one occasionally hears in French music is really foreign to it, nearly always a mark of Italian influence. True French lyricism comes surprisingly close to Rousseau's recipe for French recitative, except that he specifies 'nothing which resembles melody'. Without inverting Rousseau and suggesting that the subtlest French melody always has an element of something like recitative, one might delete that one phrase and be left with a very apt description of an intensely lyrical song such as Chausson's 'Le colibri' (Op. 2, no. 7):

Ex. 22

and quite a number of *mélodies* by Fauré and Debussy, Ravel and Poulenc.

That French instrumental melody has many affinities with French vocal melody goes without saying. Ralph Kirkpatrick has written of French keyboard-music: 'Both Couperin and Rameau, like Fauré and Debussy, are thoroughly conditioned by the nuances and inflections of spoken French. On no Western music has the influence of language been stronger.' I suggest there is a deeper affinity, in that a frequent element in both vocal and instrumental melody is the extra-musical: not emotional or metaphysical, but in the one case the text as a physical entity, in the other non-abstract conceptions. French instrumental music has no words but, as I have already remarked, it often *needs* words to complete its sense. It may consist of marches or dances, but it is seldom totally autonomous in origin and impulse. From the keyboard *ordres* of Couperin to the symphonic music of Berlioz and later nineteenth-century masters, Debussy and Ravel, Messiaen and Boulez, the proportion of such music to absolute music is markedly greater in France than anywhere else. I suggest that this close, indissoluble relationship between music and words induced by the nature of the French language has built up in France over the centuries a tradition of music fairly precise in meaning. It was of a baroque sonata that Fontenelle demanded, 'Sonate, que me veux-tu?' Whereas the German romantics found that the enchantment of instrumental music lay in its imprecision as an expressive language, the greatest French instrumental romantic was constantly seeking to equate his music with Shakespeare or Virgil. And, as a romantic composer, Berlioz himself was an isolated figure in France; the romantic age was not one of the great periods of French instrumental music.

V

THE SOCIAL FACTOR

I think we may take it as axiomatic that all music arises from and corresponds to a human need, whether the need of many or of a solitary individual. This is true of even the least human-seeming music. Electronic music, which is totally inhuman in its divorce from every element that has given any music in the world its meaning up to now, even this answers a very primitive human need: the need to experiment with whatever sound-producing agents a man has at his disposal. The first purely electronic composers—as distinct from those who used electronic sounds as an adjunct to normal musical sounds—were in the position of the first prehistoric man who got pleasure out of knocking two stones together; or, rather, they would have been if they had not had knowledge of conventional music to give them the concept of pattern. Indeed electronic musicians, despite the infinitely greater sophistication of their sound-producing apparatus, are artistically very much in the position of Stone Age man. They need not despair, for the music of Stone Age man has evolved to the music of Bach, Beethoven, and Boulez.

My real subject, however, is not so much composition as the whole practice of music at different times and in various conditions. I must not linger too long with prehistoric man, but he does stand at the beginning of things. If he howled emotionally or hit two stones together or accidentally twanged his hunting bow (the material conditions), I suppose he did it again because he liked the sound. But he must have very soon been told by his wife or friends, 'That was a nice noise. Do it again' or 'For God's sake stop that' (the earliest social pressures). We may assume that it was the range or the limitations of their means of sound-production which was a factor in determining that one great branch of the human race should develop its music to an extraordinary subtlety of melody (as in

Asia), an extraordinary subtlety of rhythm (as in Africa), or an extraordinary subtlety of simultaneous pitch-sounds (as in Europe). But different social needs and conditions must have played their parts as well. Some of these, too, were very widespread. Although we can only guess at the nature of such music in its earliest forms and though even the few fragments of instruments that survive—Queen Pu-abi's Sumerian lyres of perhaps 2500 B.C. or the Egyptian trumpets found in the tomb of Tutankhamun—are relatively modern, we know from pictures and written accounts that, whatever the nature of the music, it was associated with magic or religion, used as an aid to work, as a means of communication (sound-signals) and probably as a mnemonic aid in the transmission of long poetic narratives. These were presumably the original purposes of music in Europe, as everywhere else, though unfortunately hardly anything but religious music is documented for us in notation until the courtly songs of the twelfth century.

These songs were sophisticated in their forms and poetic ideas; the music of the Church was sophisticated in structure. Both were produced by a cultural élite and I believe it is quite false to suppose that the early development of the Western musical tradition owes anything to 'the people' in the broadest sense. (For that matter, as I have already remarked, I doubt whether it owes anything to the troubadours either.) Popular elements may have crept into religious song during its 'hidden years' and obviously at all periods minstrels and labourers, peasants and townspeople sang songs and played on instruments. But there are hardly the tiniest shreds of genuine evidence that such music played any part earlier than the fifteenth century in what we recognize as our musical heritage. Sometimes it may have amused some learned musician to borrow a scrap of popular tune or a street-cry, but it was more likely to be the other way round: a snatch of liturgical melody would be popularized, just as it is not unknown for a troubadour or *trouvère* song to be based on a liturgical clausula, as was the case with

L'altrier cuidai aber druda
tota la meillor

c'onques egusse veguda
et la belisor

in the twelfth-century *Chansonnier du Roi* on the clausula:

Ex. 23

It is altogether too easy to point to a tune in triple rhythm like
'Sumer is icumen in' and say it must have been a Wessex folk-song
(as has actually been done); folk-songs do not work in four-part
canon at the unison. Even a later tune, the famous 'L'homme armé',
often said to be a popular song, sounds to me much more like a
fifteenth-century English carol melody, anonymous but not 'popular'
art; indeed Robert Morton's *chanson* version[1] may well be the
original form:

Ex. 24

[1] In the Mellon Chansonnier at Yale.

Wemust face the fact, then, that the Western tradition began in both secular and church music in the environment of an educated class.

The earliest direct and undoubted contribution of popular music to the main tradition was made by the Florentine carnival songs of the fifteenth century. Actually the seduction of cultured Italians by popular song a little before this is attested by the words of Landini's madrigal 'Musica son'. This is the piece that heads his work in the Squarcialupi Codex where he complains—or makes Music personified complain with tears—that he sees 'intelligent people neglecting his sweet and perfect effects in favour of *frottole*'. This may well have been the consequence of the final triumph of the Italian vernacular with Dante and Petrarch. At any rate, Lorenzo the Magnificent wrote carnival songs and had them set to music appropriately popular in style by Heinrich Isaac, who was in his service during the 1480s. Similarly a little later when Isaac was court composer to Maximilian I, he made rather more sophisticated arrangements of a famous German song the words of which are attributed to the Emperor himself; 'Innsbruck, ich muss dich lassen' was certainly not a 'popular' song in origin but popular enough in nature to be handed down like a folk-song, to become a Protestant chorale as 'O Welt, ich muss dich lassen', and to end up in Bach's *Matthew Passion* as 'Ich bin's, ich sollte büssen'. Whether or not they were pressed by their patrons to interest themselves in popular music or whether, as seems likely enough, they were willingly seduced by its simple charm, the Netherland musicians in Italy and very soon learned musicians everywhere began to take notice of the music of the people. They borrowed its tunes for sophisticated treatment: in polyphonic settings, as themes for variation by the Spanish vihuelistas and English virginalists, and even by Lassus in his more scurrilous moods as themes for Masses.

(A *cantus firmus* Mass or 'parody Mass' on a secular *chanson* is one thing; a Mass on a bawdy or comic song like 'Je ne mange point du porc' is quite another.) But more important than these borrowings from popular music was the beginning of assimilation of its styles.

Several factors combined to effect a certain popularization of the European tradition after the 'waning of the Middle Ages'. Chief among them was the art of music-printing which soon spread from Venice to Germany and France and the Netherlands. Another was the increasing power and influence of the wealthy mercantile class with the emergence of a literate bourgeoisie. These seriously introduced an influential economic factor into music, so far as the composer was concerned. A connected economic history of music remains to be written but in broad terms we may put it that up to this point the only people who were financially concerned with music were those whose music was ephemeral: the humble performers, the minstrels who practised private enterprise and who ranked in the eyes of respectable citizens with beggars and vagabonds, and the town-musicians, waits and *Stadtpfeifer* and trumpeters who organized themselves into guilds and established their financial rights and privileges. But the creators of enduring music were either nobles or the rare lay professional musicians who formed part of their households or, far more often, they were ecclesiastics. For many centuries the question of making money by performing in church never arose; the clergy sang or played primarily as churchmen rather than as musicians. And so composers composed; they were primarily choirmen or instrumentalists and when, in the course of time, they began to be paid they were paid for performing, not for composing. We may be confident that Perotinus was not paid a sou for his four-part organa any more than an English or Scottish monk was paid for copying them. A distinguished career could be rewarded by the grant of benefices, and service in princely chapels brought financial bonuses as well as other marks of favour. Probably John Aleyn received something special from Edward III of England for his great Order of the Garter motet, 'Sub Arturo', but we don't know. So much was on a personal basis. And of course the valuable ring or diamond-studded snuffbox remained royal currency for the payment of musicians right down to the time of Liszt.

Even more frustrating is our ignorance of the financial side of music-publishing in its early days. How did Petrucci pay the composers whose works he printed in the first decade of the sixteenth century? Probably not at all; they would most likely have had to be content—like capitalist authors in Russia today—with the knowledge that their work was getting more widely known. After a time a few composers, Susato at Antwerp, Georg Rhaw at Wittenberg, Morley in London, were astute enough to become publishers themselves, but naturally they were a very tiny minority.

* * *

Publication—in the original literal sense of 'making public'—gradually brought to the surface a complex of inter-related issues which are very much with us to this day and have both reflected and influenced the course of Western music. They may be considered in relation to two main questions: how is a composer to be recompensed for composition, as distinct from his other activities? and what is the composer's relation to a large anonymous public of performers and listeners? For the composer before 1500, churchman or layman in the service of a court or princely chapel, writing for a small group of performers of whom he was one and to satisfy the tastes and needs of his master and a circle with which he was equally familiar, these questions did not arise. It is curious to reflect that down to the time of the French Revolution there were still some composers—I suppose Haydn was one of the last—for whom they arose only marginally. But by that time these were the exceptions. At first the church and court musicians of the sixteenth century were in the great majority and could go on composing in the old way with a lordly disregard for any wider public that might want to buy their music; but there were now other composers: the Lutheran composers of four-part chorales, and the Calvinist composers of four-part settings of the Psalms in metrical vernacular, more for private devotion in the home than for use in church, which were written and sung all over Europe from France and Scotland to Poland, and taken up by Catholics as well as Protestants. The composers of this domestic religious music knew they were writing for a large, anonymous but intelligent and literate middle-class public and this certainly affected their approach, though, not only then but for a very long time after, they could make money from their compositions only by selling the manuscripts outright to a publisher. Probably the publisher actually took the initiative and thus became a stimulating factor. Georg Rhaw presumably commissioned work from his composers. But even before this, publishers had known how to create a market. The very earliest of them, Petrucci, had been in business only five or six years when, under pressure from threatened rivals, he began publishing lute-transcriptions made by his fellow-townsman Francesco Spinaccino and then *frottole* with the lower parts arranged for lute, for the convenience of singers who wanted to accompany themselves. This was surely a pure business venture; it was marked by a lowering of Petrucci's original standard of printing; and no doubt Francesco Spinaccino and Francesco the Bosnian (were they the same person?) were hired by Petrucci to do the work for him. Attaingnant in Paris may or may not himself have been the anonymous arranger of the lute transcriptions—for instrument only and for voice with lute accompaniment—of the songs he also published in four-part versions. And was he the author of the famous instruction book?[2] More probably he had a composer-editor in his printing office; it certainly seems that he had a tame poet, no less than Clément Marot. And in a different way, before the century was out, Thomas Morley was cashing in on the English mania for everything Italian by composing (or sometimes half-plagiarizing) and publishing Italian-style pieces with anglicized Italian names, madrigals, canzonets and ballets, and—a real commercial masterstroke—putting out a book[3] which indicated that it was shameful for a gentleman not to be able to sing a part in music of this kind at sight or at the least talk knowledgeably about music.

[2] *Très brève et familière introduction pour entendre et apprendre par soy-mesme à jouer toutes chansons réduictes en la tablature du lutz* (Paris, 1529).
[3] *A Plaine and Easie Introduction to Practicall Musicke* (London, 1597).

Elizabethan England may not have been quite the land of song it has sometimes been assumed to be, on the strength of Morley's insinuation, but there is plenty of evidence that music was widely practised and enjoyed not only by the aristocracy but by the educated middle class. And the same was true more or less all over Europe. Ceremonial madrigals would be composed in Italy for princely weddings, and sumptuous polychoral Masses for coronations and other state occasions; but lute ayres were not the peculiar property of fops at Court, madrigals and *chansons* and religious part-songs were sung, and instrumental consort music was played, in middle-class homes. This new broad public for printed music had a gradual effect on the evolution of the Western tradition that was much more important than the impact of popular music itself. In Germany the two more or less coincided, for (as we have seen) popular song had been at the very basis of German music from the days of the early organ tablatures, where the arrangements of fairly humble mono-phonic *Lieder* sit side by side with transcriptions of courtly Burgun-dian *chansons*. When a new highly sophisticated form of music appeared it was soon popularized, as we see in the case of opera. There have been few forms more artificial and intellectual than opera as conceived by the Florentine Camerata, but Italian courts took it up and mixed it with elements of such essentially courtly entertainments as the masque and the ballet: a first step in populari-zation. And in less than thirty years there was an opera-house in Venice to which the paying public were admitted to help defray expenses: a second and much bigger step.

There already we see foreshadowed the pattern that was to be followed by Western music from the early days of its lessening dependence on church and court right down to the present. There was one kind of music largely performed by amateurs of varying degrees of cultivation, mainly in their own homes, which again covered the whole range from the palatial to the bourgeois. The more this kind of music widened its scope, the more it developed popular forms and often depreciated its values; it is useless to pretend that the English glee and part-song at their best ever reached anything like the artistic level of the madrigal at its best, or that the

German *Liedertafel* type of chorus has contributed immortal pages to the German heritage. (It certainly contributed to the beginnings of romantic opera but its offering was sadly undistinguished.) This area of music included the so-called drawing-room ballad and salon-music for piano. But let us remember that it also included the *Lieder* of Schubert and Schumann, Brahms and Hugo Wolf, the people who played string quartets in their own homes and sang in choral societies, and the people who, as someone has said, 'won the battle for *Tristan* on the pianos of Germany'. These are the people who, until the coming of the phonograph record and radio, made up what we loosely call 'the musical public' of Europe and America, and these are typical of the kinds of music they performed for their own satisfaction.

But there was another kind of music in which this public, which in the early seventeenth century was still a new public, took no active part but an increasingly important passive part, music to which they only listened. (Nowadays most of them 'only listen' to every kind of music, and that attitude too has its reasons and its consequences.) Its earliest important forms were the music of public ceremonial (church music that was still supposed to glorify God but really glorified the ruler or the state, music that was calculated to attract listeners rather than worshippers), and above all opera. Opera was to become by far the most important in many obvious ways and also in some that perhaps we hardly recognize. The Church continued to look after its own music in the same old way, no matter whether it was only pseudo-liturgical or frankly non-liturgical (as early oratorio was, or eighteenth-century Passion music.) But opera was secular and when it passed from the domain of princes and cardinals, as it so quickly did, the question of finance reared its ugly head. The members of the Venetian oligarchy who opened the Teatro di San Cassiano in 1637 were not contemplating a really popular commercial theatre like London's Globe, but on the other hand they were not absolute princes to whom money was of no account where private pleasures were concerned. They were very grand and wealthy merchants, a social and cultural élite who knew what they wanted but had no intention of ruining themselves in the process of getting it. Opera has always been extremely expensive and their solution of the problem of paying for it took two familiar forms: they cut down the expenses as far as possible and they spread the financial load by allowing the general public to share both it and the enjoyment of opera. One way in which they cut down expenses was by reducing the size of the orchestra, as may be seen by comparing the extremely modest orchestra of Monteverdi's last, Venetian operas or Cavalli's with the extravagantly lavish one of *Orfeo*, for which the Duke of Mantua footed the bill in 1607. I am not suggesting that this was a bad thing—*L'Incoronazione di Poppea* is arguably a greater masterpiece than *Orfeo*—any more than I deplore the injection of lyrical elements into the severely intellectual opera of the Camerata, without which opera would never have achieved life, much less popularity. I mention the reduced size of the early Venetian opera orchestra only as a striking instance of economic pressure on an art-form.

The pattern of events here, a wider public following the lead of a cultural élite, has become as familiar as the élite's financial methods. Italy has a three-hundred-year tradition of popular opera, but Italian opera did not come into existence as a result of popular demand. The renewal of art, the fresh lead in art, nearly always comes from what I have called a dynamic nucleus, professionally or socially influential persons or groups. But a tradition can be established in the post-Renaissance world only if the lead arouses public support; the public will follow a lead only if it wants to and as far as it wants to. It can be led but not driven. It may begin to follow for the wrong reason and go on for the right one; it may begin by wanting to be on the cultural band-waggon and then go on genuinely to enjoy the band. It may, of course, end by paying the band and steering the waggon, which is what happened with Italian opera later in the seventeenth century when public demand for song rather than dramatic recitative, and composers' more than willingness to supply the demand, led to the excesses of the *da capo* aria and the reduction of the dramatic element to so many formulae. It was surely the taste of the groundlings that led to the spending of money on sensational scenic effects. (Late seventeenth-century opera was in some respects the equivalent of the twentieth-century film.) *Opera buffa*, which arrived on the scene originally in the form of comic interludes to relieve the boredom of *opera seria*, was an obvious bid for popular support. But *opera seria* itself was, quite as much as *opera buffa*, an art-form conditioned by the demands of the audience —though in the first place of a cultivated audience.

* * *

The different ways in which opera was diffused throughout Europe depended almost entirely on social or even political conditions. In France it was established in a specifically French form under Louis XIV and in a grand central institution which has experienced all sorts of splendours and miseries and some changes of name, but has survived all revolutions. It began as a royal opera and has always remained a state institution. In Germany the story was quite different. First, Italian opera in its pure form was brought as a new and fashionable exotic art to the courts of Vienna and Munich and Dresden, and then naturally spread to those numerous petty courts which were long the symbols of Germany's political weakness but the sources of much cultural strength. Each court-opera, large or small, attracted musicians, brought into being an orchestra and served as a growing-point for musical activity, whereas France, with only one royal opera, had only one real growing-point. The special cult of Italian opera lingered on in Vienna and Prague, Berlin and Dresden, long after German opera had developed its own being. But it is not without significance that truly German opera was developed out of the Italian in North Germany, in a city that was the German equivalent of Venice, a wealthy mercantile port, the Free City of Hamburg.

The case of England was very different again, and the failure of opera really to take root there had disastrous consequences for English music. The reasons for the failure have been variously explained. One plausible suggestion is that, after Shakespeare, poetic drama was so firmly entrenched that opera stood no chance of rivalling it; certainly there were misguided attempts to mate the two. But I think the reasons go rather deeper. The new Italian recitative style reached England quite quickly, by the second decade of the century, and was employed at once in that typical form of court entertainment, the masque. But the essential nature of opera as drama was never properly grasped. When *The Siege of Rhodes*, the first English opera, was produced under the Puritan Common-wealth, the music was supplied by a whole committee of composers, five of them, in itself an indication that opera was not conceived as a unified work of art. The Restoration brought to the throne a monarch whose tastes were more French than Italian and the fashionable French models of the first fourteen or fifteen years of Charles II's reign were the *opéras-ballets* which must have confirmed the English conception of opera as a hotch-potch of poetic play, masque and ballet. But the theatre was still a commercial theatre, not a royal one; the king patronized the actresses rather than the theatre as such. The only true English operas, which did not appear until the 1680s, Blow's *Venus and Adonis* (characteristically described as a 'masque') and Purcell's *Dido and Aeneas*, are more Lullyan than Italian. And both were miniature works performed by amateurs, by schoolgirls. When Italian opera did reach Britain in a big way, and under Handel and his rivals dominated London musical life for a quarter of a century, it was not adopted and naturalized. It was patronized by rival court factions and supported by cultural snobs, but its absur-dities were mocked at by our sturdy, rational intellectuals like Addison and caricatured in *The Beggar's Opera*. In fact the only native forms it generated were the ballad-operas and pasticcio-operas, and the best a philosophical Englishman can do is to reflect that the ballad-opera was a parent of the German *Singspiel* and so contributed ultimately to produce *The Magic Flute*.

The most serious consequences of this attitude to opera went much deeper. Opera was confined to London; there were no travelling opera-companies as in Italy and Germany. And even in London it remained a purely commercial affair, without official princely support such as it had in France, Italy, Germany, and Russia. By this time opera, with the orchestral repertoire that grew up around it under its stimulus, constituted the most important element in the main stream of European music; yet it was beyond the ken of British

95

musicians and music-lovers outside London, while even Londoners knew it mostly in feeble or garbled forms which persisted well into the nineteenth century under Henry Bishop. In place of the numerous composers and conductors working in the opera-houses all over Italy and Germany, British music—particularly in the provinces—was directed and influenced almost entirely by church musicians, cathedral organists and their kind, who were ignorant of opera and generally uninterested in the new forms of orchestral music. Even orchestras in the provinces were only *ad hoc* collections of players, assembled for particular occasions. The organists were competent in their own field, but even in that they were conservative; their church music was never revitalized from the main stream, never ran the slightest danger of becoming operatic like Mozart's or symphonic like Haydn's. Beyond liturgical music, British composers were obsessed with Handel's splendid but fatal legacy of English oratorio. It was not through his overpowering genius that Handel did such harm to English music, as has sometimes been alleged, but through the diversion of creative effort into a form no one but he mastered with complete success and in which neither Haydn nor Mendelssohn reached the height of his powers.

It is hardly possible to exaggerate the importance of opera in the total Western tradition, not only for its own sake and on account of its contributions generally—its forms and styles and techniques—but for its influence on the organization of musical life. In no other field is the composer more immediately involved with society, more at its mercy, more able to influence it. By its nature, open to all the other arts, opera absorbs and reflects the general cultural tendencies of its place and period much more readily than any other form of music. (Consider the close relationship of Meyerbeerian grand opera to the Paris of Louis Philippe and the Second Empire, of Wagner's work to the grandiose, self-consciously Teutonic Germany after 1871.) And from quite early days opera has spawned other forms. The cantatas of Alessandro Grandi, who seems to have been the first to use the term, were based on the same plan as Monteverdi's 'Qual onor' (Example 12) with its repeated bass, and by the end of the seventeenth century all the major vocal forms were either modelled on opera forms or strongly influenced by opera: the French chamber cantata, and above all oratorio which had been patterned on opera from Carissimi onward and retained markedly operatic elements even in non-dramatic works like *Messiah* and *The Creation*. Even church music could be operatic. From Schütz in some of his *geistliche Konzerte*, for instance, 'Eile mich, Gott, zu erretten':[4]

Ex. 25

through Bach's Passions to Mozart's church music, German religious music, Catholic and Protestant alike and the greatest as well as the mediocre, was based on the forms of opera or permeated by its styles.

The instrumental forms which derived from opera were, so to speak, extensions of it for the sake of the same public: the passive public that paid to listen to music. In the eighteenth century the three-movement Italian opera overture became so popular as an instrumental form that it provided a general pattern for the Vivaldian concerto and, more important, was given an independent existence as the concert symphony. In the early nineteenth century history really did for once repeat itself, and the one-movement opera overture also achieved independence as the 'concert overture' and

[4] From the *Kleine geistliche Konzerte* (1636).

hence gave birth to the symphonic poem. (We must remember that Liszt invented the term rather than the thing; most of his earlier 'symphonic poems'—*Ce qu'on entend sur la montagne, Tasso, Les Préludes, Prometheus, Festklänge*—were in the first place theatre or concert overtures and originally actually so called.) The classical orchestra also proceeded indirectly from opera, for the international popularity of the concert symphony in the early eighteenth century, with the publication of sets of printed parts, spelled the end of the baroque orchestra, the miscellaneous collection of instruments a composer happened to have at hand; instead it brought about a basic standardization of four-part strings with a pair of, often unspecified, woodwind. And many innovations in the standard orchestra were made first in opera. Mozart transferred trombones from the church to the opera-house in *Idomeneo, Don Giovanni* and *The Magic Flute* not for their sound alone but because of their associations with religion, awe and solemnity. And from the opera-house they passed before very long to the concert orchestra. The giant orchestra which Berlioz employed in his symphonies, with such luxuries as four bassoons, was unprecedented in the concert-hall, but it was the normal orchestra of the Paris Opéra of the time, originally built up to meet the demands of the spectacular scores of Spontini.

I need say nothing of the influence of Wagner's orchestra on the concert orchestra since his day, both in size and in its expressive techniques. But his non-orchestral expressive techniques, as in harmony, have had even more influence on the language of music, an influence that would have annoyed rather than flattered him. He once remarked to Edward Dannreuther that

> when occasion offered [he] could venture to depict strange and even terrible things in music, because the action rendered such things comprehensible; but music apart from the drama cannot risk this, for fear of becoming grotesque.[5]

He went on to say, 'I am afraid my scores will be of little use to composers of instrumental music.' But there, of course, he was quite mistaken. Even in his lifetime composers of instrumental music, as

[5] *Grove's Dictionary* (second edition), ed. J. A. Fuller Maitland, V, p. 414.

he grumbled to Wolzogen, had 'learned from me how to write symphony without drama and thus without comprehensibility'.[6] He was only attributing to his own case a process that has gone on more or less throughout the history of opera: the enrichment of European music in general, even the most seemingly absolute, by expressive means first employed by operatic composers and only then transferred to other areas. As Mahler put it to a correspondent in 1896,

> Now the symphonic composer will justifiably and consciously seize upon the means of expression which music has won through Wagner.[7]

The social paradox of opera is that, while it is the most expensive way of performing music, hardly ever self-supporting, essentially an art for the rich, it long appealed to the widest public. As Chaykovsky once wrote:

> [Opera] alone gives one the means to communicate with the *masses* of the public. My *Manfred* [Symphony] will be played once or twice, then laid aside for Heaven knows how long, and no one but the handful of connoisseurs who go to symphony concerts will know it. Opera, and opera alone, brings you close to people, makes your name familiar to the real public, makes you the property not merely of separate little circles but—with luck—of the whole people.[8]

Any nineteenth-century Italian or French composer would have said the same, and probably most Germans, though after Chaykovsky's day popular symphony concerts began to alter the picture even before the coming of the phonograph record and the radio. This other form of mass, passive listening, the public concert, began, like opera, among small cultural élites, the London music clubs and semi-private concerts like La Pouplinière's in Paris, expanding with the passage of time to take in a wider subscribing

[6] Hans von Wolzogen, *Erinnerungen an Richard Wagner* (Leipzig, 1891), p. 30.
[7] Letter to Max Marschalk, 26 March 1896, in *Gustav Mahler Briefe: 1879–1911* (Berlin, 1924), pp. 187–8.
[8] Letter to Nadezhda von Meck, 27 September 1885.

public. But it long appealed to a more specialized audience than the opera audience. If you went to a concert there was nothing to do but listen to the music; you did not go to be entertained by a spectacle as well—indeed two spectacles, one on the stage, the other in the boxes, the tastes of whose occupants were often reflected in the work itself, its production and its performance. (The social history of opera is another task which still awaits its author.) But the concert-world itself was long dominated by opera in ways that are easily forgotten today. The operatic excerpt in the orchestral programme or the aria in the vocal recital was normal in the nineteenth century, very unusual today. Operatic fantasias were important items in piano recitals from the earliest days of those institutions, which were only just pre-Victorian, and they died out only with Busoni or thereabouts. The non-opera-going public reached by opera-music was vastly wider even than that. In England, at any rate, in my boyhood, arrangements of opera overtures and potpourris on opera-tunes appeared in every outdoor band programme and in Italy not so very long ago it was possible to hear a complete act of a Verdi opera played out of doors by a wind-band—naturally with audience participation. Operetta, musical comedy and the 'musical' are essentially only successive stages in the popularization of opera.

* * *

The financing of opera has always been a serious problem, but so far as the composer was concerned opera was the most remunerative form of composition. Where purely commercial theatres were involved, he might even have a direct share in the venture as Handel did in London. In any case he could sell or hire his score and other performing material directly to the theatre, or he could collect a fee for the right of performance. Practices differed so much even in the same country and at the same time that it is impossible to generalize; for instance, in Germany in the middle of the last century most opera-houses paid a lump sum for the right to perform a new work as many times as they wanted to, but the Royal Opera at Berlin paid a royalty on each performance. Publication was a matter of secondary importance and in early days might not happen at all. Here again practice differed widely. Monteverdi's *Orfeo* was handsomely published and soon went into a second edition; his later operas were not. If an opera was composed for some grand occasion, like *Orfeo* or Cesti's *Pomo d'oro*, ducal or royal or imperial money would pay for a commemorative edition. But in the eighteenth century volumes of 'favourite airs' from operas, if not complete vocal scores, must have produced further rewards for the composer—provided he took care that his work was not pirated by some unscrupulous publisher. A successful opera-composer, a Rossini, a Verdi or a Puccini, might make a living, and something rather better, from composition alone; but neither Mozart nor Wagner, who were by no means unsuccessful, managed to do so.

In other fields it was quite impossible. As with an opera, a composer could sell his songs or sonatas outright to a publisher, but usually for a miserable sum. He could perform and so both publicize his compositions and use them as a draw. He could take a conducting post at a theatre—if he was lucky, at a state theatre. He could teach or even become a newspaper critic. His real problem was to achieve a balance in time and energy between these activities and composition. He was sometimes helped, and still is, by survivals of patronage: the dedication that might bring a generous gift in return, the subsidies of wealthy friends which Beethoven, Wagner and Chaykovsky in their various ways contrived to attract. It was only by combining some or all of these methods that a composer could contrive to live. But he had to be enormously successful—that is, enormously popular— before he could hope to live by composition alone. The very idea of being able to do so would hardly have occurred to a musician before Beethoven's day; it was the romantic conception of the creative artist as a being apart, a cultural hero or demigod, that made it irksome and rather shameful to write *pièces d'occasion* and 'popular' music, even such charming and skilful things as the Sullivan operettas.

The conception of a creative artist as a superior being who ought to be free from social pressures may not have originated with composers but they naturally found it easily acceptable. It began to be modified after the First World War, partly as a result of the efforts of

Hindemith and others to revive the older conception of the composer as craftsman. Few during the last forty years would have scorned to write film-music. The type who considered that society owed him a living just because he was a composer is now nearly, though not quite, extinct.

The consequences of that attitude have been unfortunate for music itself. The romantic composer's contempt for popular music opened a cleft between 'serious' and 'popular' that did not exist when Handel wrote songs for the London pleasure-garden concerts and Mozart and Schubert composed real, not idealized, dance-music. Quite a number of composers—for instance, Ives and Copland and Gershwin in their totally different ways—have tried to close that cleft, but it remains open and actually grows wider. The 'serious' composer has withdrawn more and more out of touch with the wider public; he no longer wants to share his personal emotions with it, as the romantics did, much less to entertain it as the classics did. And what I have called the élite public, the hard core of which is often quite as serious as he is, is less able to follow him and so to disseminate its interest, much less its enthusiasm, in those ever widening circles which used to form the normal pattern of musical diffusion. The élite itself has largely disintegrated. The hard core of enthusiasts for advanced music consists mainly of intellectuals, who are not as a class outstandingly wealthy. On the other hand, the wealthy public seems to be generally more interested in supporting institutions which no longer appeal very strongly to the *avant-garde* musician: the opera-house and the big symphonic orchestra. It is a tragic impasse: on the one hand composers contemptuous of traditional forms and media, on the other a public which prefers to spend its money on preserving tradition in the wrong way, by petrifying it. The *avant-garde* composer thus finds himself willy-nilly in the position of a rebel against the social culture represented by that public, and he is now reacting by experimenting with totally new musics conceived for a totally new society in which the élite public may consist of technologists uninterested in traditional cultural values.

In the meantime different countries are in different ways seeking solutions to this problem of music and society as it confronts us here and now, the problem of preserving alive and (it is to be hoped) continuing our musical tradition in our existing society. The nub of the problem is: How, and how much, is society willing to provide substitutes for the princely and ecclesiastical employers and wealthy patrons of the past? Even with the help of modern copyright laws and performing-right agreements, most composers need, not complete support by a patron but occasional financial help to free their minds for some major piece of work. In the United States I believe the wealthy patron still exists, though his function has been largely assumed by the great charitable foundations. I am not sure to what extent the Federal or State governments or the municipalities oblige the ordinary citizen to contribute by taxation to the support of musicians or those institutions, like opera-houses and orchestras, which—like art-galleries and museums—are not viable commercial undertakings. In Britain, where the wealthy individual patron has been nearly taxed out of existence, the Government does this, though not directly as in France through a Ministry of Culture. It sets aside a proportion of the nation's annual expenditure to be administered by an independent Arts Council which subsidizes all forms of art. The Council has representative professional advisory committees and works in a characteristically pragmatic English way very much as a patron in the past would probably have done. It spends a very large amount of money in support of a great international opera-house and a more modest English-language opera in London and does what it can to help operatic enterprises elsewhere. It helps the symphony orchestras, of which London has too many and the rest of Britain too few. And it will give a deserving but commercially unsuccessful composer six months' or a year's financial security to concentrate on a special piece of work. The British Broadcasting Corporation is not an agent of the Government like the Arts Council, though it is financed by a licensing system operated by a Government department. It too is a patron, as well as the most important employer of musicians in Britain. Much of its patronage is 'hidden' in the form of broadcasting fees paid to festivals, to groups specializing in the performance of old music or very advanced music, but it also commissions compositions. There is some municipal help for music too; provincial cities fortunate enough to have their own symphony orchestras usually contribute towards their support.

By comparison with this rather complicated and seemingly haphazard way of doing things, the Soviet Russian system has a beautiful simplicity. The state recognizes the value of music to society: accordingly it pays for the opera establishments, the orchestras, and so on, the conservatories of music, the publication of music, and the subsistence of composers. This is a magnificent and munificent conception, but it has a flaw. The Soviet State believes, logically enough in view of its premises, that the composer as a member of a society that supports him should write for his fellow-citizens music that is not too intellectual, not too strange in idiom for them to enjoy. But the interpretation of that criterion has been entrusted to unmusical Party leaders and timorous or time-serving musicians-in-office, a 'dynamic nucleus' of a new and regrettable kind. The nucleus has exerted its power and, by and large, Soviet composers have been content to submit to its pressures, with only isolated gestures of self-assertion from well-established figures and quite recently from the young generation; on the other hand the Soviet public would not fill concert-halls to listen to the music of 'Socialist realism' if it disliked this kind of music with its unadventurous idioms and its mildly national flavour. The great public, Communist and bourgeois alike, never tires of the familiar. The general result of Soviet Russia's loss of contact with the main stream of Western music through over-preoccupation with the social-political content of music has been all too closely comparable with that of the English over-valuation of the social-religious content of music in the century after Handel. Both produced music that is provincial in the worst sense. From which we may draw the lesson that, while social environment is always a formative and determinant of musical tradition and often a stimulant, it can also be an unfortunate sedative.

VI

TRADITION AND THE
INDIVIDUAL GENIUS

Once, after listening to the *Meistersinger* overture, Nietzsche wrote of it in *Jenseits von Gut und Böse*[1] as 'splendid, sumptuous, weighty and late art which can proudly postulate two centuries of music for its comprehension.' And T. S. Eliot, in an essay[2] whose title I have shamelessly borrowed and adapted, has suggested that we do wrong, when we praise a poet,

> to insist ... upon those aspects of his work in which he least resembles anyone else. ... We shall often find that not only the best, but the most individual parts of his work may be those in which the dead poets, his ancestors, assert their immortality most vigorously. And I do not mean the impressionable period of adolescence, but the period of full maturity. ... If the only form of tradition ... consisted in following the ways of the immediate generation before us in a blind or timid adherence to its successes, 'tradition' should positively be discouraged ... [but] tradition is a matter of much wider significance. ... It involves, in the first place, the historical sense ... which is a sense of the timeless as well as of the temporal and of the timeless and of the temporal together. [This] is what makes a writer traditional. And it is at the same time what makes a writer most acutely conscious of his place in time, of his contemporaneity. No poet, no artist of any sort, has his complete meaning alone. His significance, his appreciation is the appreciation of his relation to the dead poets and artists.

So far it is easy to agree with Eliot. To have 'a sense of the timeless as well as of the temporal and of the timeless and of the temporal

[1] Leipzig, 1886, p. 195.
[2] 'Tradition and the Individual Talent' in *The Sacred Wood* (London, 1920).

together' is one of the most precious gifts a music critic, as well as a literary critic, can possess. To listen to a late Beethoven string quartet timelessly as a thing in itself, purely as an aesthetic or emotional experience, is wonderful. To hear it in relation to its age, to the rest of Beethoven's music, to all the string quartets written before it, is fascinating. To apprehend it to the full one needs to be able to do both. And when Eliot proceeds to examine the relation of the poet to the past, it is still possible to agree that much of what he says may be applied with equal force to the composer:

> The poet must be very conscious of the main current, which does not at all flow invariably through the most distinguished reputations. He must be quite aware of the obvious fact that art never improves, but that the material of art is never quite the same. He must be aware that the mind of Europe—the mind of his own country—a mind which he learns in time to be much more important than his own private mind—is a mind which changes, and that this change is a development which abandons nothing *en route*, which does not superannuate either Shakespeare, or Homer, or the rock drawing of the Magdalenian draughtsmen.

It is when Eliot goes on to develop his doctrine or, as he calls it, his 'programme for the *métier* of poetry', that one perceives a parting of the ways ahead. It is a programme for a learned poetry:

> The poet must develop or procure the consciousness of the past and . . . should continue to develop this consciousness throughout his career.

There must be

> a continual surrender of himself as he is at the moment to something which is more valuable. The progress of an artist is a continual self-sacrifice, a continual extinction of personality.

The ways of literature and music part here because men of letters have always, except in the Dark Ages and early Middle Ages, been conscious of their past, even if they knew it only by distorted hearsay; for more than half a millennium now they have been acutely aware of their heritage from Greece and Rome down, with gaps of unavoidable ignorance, to their own day. This certainly cannot be said of musicians. It is only within the last two hundred years that musicians have been aware of much more than the music of today and yesterday. If names of musicians of a more distant past were remembered at all, they were figures of myth, hardly more real than Orpheus, lost in a haze where Dunstable could actually be confused with St. Dunstan.[3] Books of plainsong were preserved because plainsong was in constant use, but in the Middle Ages an old musical style was as obsolete as last year's feminine fashions are today; its compositions were valueless and the parchment on which it was written might be used in monasteries for book-binding. When manuscripts *were* preserved it was probably because of the beauty of the codex as itself a work of art or because people and institutions do hoard things without ever looking at them—because they don't like throwing anything away.

It was probably through the work of historians, beginning with Burney and Hawkins in the 1770s, that musicians first realized that their art had an interesting past that stretched back even beyond Palestrina. In Germany this new historicism was partly a by-product of romanticism, with its fascination for a half-fictitious Middle Age. Justus Thibaut's propaganda for Palestrina[4] was in step with the work of the so-called 'Nazarene' painters. Even Bach had to be revived when he was only eighty years dead. It is true that Mozart in the 1780s had been excited by the discovery of the *Forty-eight* and by hearing 'Singet dem Herrn'; but in 1789 'Singet dem Herrn' was only half-a-century old, less ancient than *Pierrot Lunaire* and the *Rite of Spring* are to us. Beethoven and some of his contemporaries also valued the *Forty-eight*. But when Mendelssohn gave the famous Berlin performance of the *Matthew Passion* in 1829, he had to do it in a version that was acceptable to an audience of his day. The very idea of performing really old music was novel. We must not be misled by the foundation of a society which gave Ancient Concerts in London in 1776, the year of Hawkins's *History* and Burney's

[3] e.g. by Marpurg, *Abhandlung von der Fuge*, II (Berlin, 1754).
[4] *Über Reinheit der Tonkunst* (Heidelberg, 1825).

first volume; it is true the society did something to revive or keep alive the best work of the madrigalists and Purcell, but its real criterion of antiquity was that a work must be at least twenty years old. As for the performance of music of real antiquity, long after Arnold Dolmetsch and others had begun to bring sixteenth-century music to life, the music of the Middle Ages had to wait till the Vienna Congress of 1927 where Perotinus was travestied by Rudolf von Ficker. Yet we must remember it was due to the Mendelssohns and the Fickers that musicians began to realize that fairly old, even extremely old, music could be living and exciting art. So long as it was in the hands only of historians and palaeographers it had lacked the breath of life.

This is all very different from the world of literature, where not only the writers themselves but a very large proportion of their readers have long been conscious of a tradition reaching far back in time, with all its explicit and implicit values, and have even known a good deal of it at first hand. With music there has been a vast gradual accretion of the values of tradition, but it has been almost entirely unconscious; the field of awareness was generally limited to no more than a generation back and so far as it took note of explicit values did so only to reject them. The two centuries of music which the *Meistersinger* overture could postulate for its comprehension had saturated the minds and formed the tastes and powers of apprehension of the German musical public over that period, but the early listeners to Wagner can have been conscious of only a small proportion of it. Wagner himself did possess some historical sense; he was always ready to appeal to the example of Gluck; and he early recognized the value to the creative artist of tradition in Eliot's sense. In a letter written during his first stay in Paris[5] he said of Berlioz:

Among the French [he] stands so completely *alone* that, being without the necessary basis, he is obliged to feel his way in a fantastic labyrinth which makes a *beautiful* development of his enormous powers extremely difficult, indeed will perhaps make it

[5] To Ferdinand Heine, 27 March 1841. *Sämtliche Briefe*, I (Leipzig, 1968), p. 465.

impossible. He is and remains an isolated phenomenon, although he is French in the full sense of the word. We Germans are fortunate; for we have our Mozart and Beethoven in our blood, and know how we can let our pulses beat. But Berlioz has no predecessors and is damned to an everlasting fever.

He was wrong about Berlioz's lack of musical ancestry, as other critics have been since. At least one element in it played a not unimportant part in his own: the operas of Spontini. Berlioz's isolation from the other Frenchmen of his day was due partly to his very fidelity to the Gluckist tradition, partly to his continuance of it through symphony rather than through opera, for which he lacked the essential chameleon gift of the true musical dramatist. (He lacked it so completely that Joseph Kerman in his classic study of *Opera as Drama* has not thought it necessary even to mention his name.) Yet, as Wagner said, he was 'French in the full sense of the word': French in the classic restraint, almost to the point of dryness, of much of his utterance even in some of the extravagant works of his romantic youth, much more in later ones like *L'Enfance du Christ* and *Les Troyens*; French in the ease with which he could fall victim to the glorious and grandiose; French in the fineness and precision of his line-drawing and the transparency of his texture; French above all in the importance of literary and pictorial elements in his music. With all his exquisite sensitivity to timbre, one sometimes feels that his—more even than Wagner's—was an artistic genius that fortunately happened to choose music as the medium through which to manifest itself. Most of the great masters are inconceivable as anything but musicians.

If Wagner was wrong about Berlioz, he was right about the value of the German tradition—of which he was particularly conscious in 1841 after a period of apostasy. It is curious that he speaks of *Mozart* and Beethoven; one thinks of other and lesser German composers of whom Wagner had more in his blood than Mozart. But in a letter one does not always choose one's words with care, and perhaps at the moment Wagner was subconsciously associating the D minor of the Dutchman's damnation with the D minor of Don Giovanni's, as well as with the D minor of the Ninth Symphony (which he associated with Goethe's Faust)[6] and the D minor of his own *Faust* Overture. No composer earlier than Wagner had had anything like his historical sense, had been (in Eliot's phrase) 'so acutely conscious of his place in time, of his contemporaneity', or had had so keen an 'appreciation of his relation to the dead poets and artists'. At the most they had been conscious only of their immediate predecessors and models and perhaps the technical procedures of an older master here and there. I have just mentioned the D minor associations that were accumulating in Wagner's mind (and let us remember how the D minor storm of the *Dutchman* overture dies away in the storm of the opening of *Die Walküre*). I have already remarked that 'we cannot hear B minor without our subconscious being stirred by memories of the Kyrie of Bach's Mass, the first movement of the Unfinished Symphony, and Chaykovsky's *Pathétique*'. But this is our sense of it, not those particular composers' sense. It is possible that Chaykovsky, beginning a symphony in gloomy depths, was guided to B minor by unconscious memory of Schubert; but we can be quite confident that Schubert did not know the B minor Mass, though he *could* have known it, for it was published a year or two before he composed the Unfinished; even so, it would hardly have carried any aroma of associations for him. Our modern sense of B minorness is partly an unconscious accumulation of association but it is heightened and enriched, not only because more and more music has been written in B minor but because we, the listeners, have developed this historical sense.

It is a sense that greatly enhances the listeners' experience, but Eliot does not say that 'the *reader* must develop or procure the consciousness of the past and . . . should continue to develop this consciousness'. He says 'the *poet*', and I question whether this imperative bears translation into musical terms. 'The composer must develop the consciousness of the past'? There must be 'a continual surrender of himself as he is at the moment to something which is more valuable'? This is a very personal and questionable

---

[6] See his programme-note on the Symphony, *Gesammelte Schriften und Dichtungen,* II, p. 56.

doctrine of poetry, and it becomes even more dubious if applied to music. The historical sense has appeared so comparatively recently among composers that it is not easy to find examples of its effect on their music. We must rule out the element of eighteenth-century pastiche in Chaykovsky and Strauss and Stravinsky; this is the assumption of a special style for a specific purpose; there is an element of play in it, a putting on of a masquerade dress. It is a little like borrowing an actual folk-melody. Perhaps the only genuine case of musical historicism has been the cult of Bach. When a nineteenth-century composer was conscious of Beethoven—and most of the major ones were conscious of him nearly all the time— this was natural enough: the heroes of the generation before are always there to be followed or rebelled against. But when Mendelssohn and Schumann and their successors studied and imitated Bach, they were doing something that had probably never been done before: deliberately turning back to a past age and a long outmoded style. They did it in different ways and achieved different degrees of success. Mendelssohn, Schumann and Brahms all composed more or less Bachian fugues, but whereas Mendelssohn sometimes applied Bachian devices superficially and without much relevance, as when he adopted the Passion use of the chorale in *St. Paul*, and Brahms was content to romanticize the chorale prelude, Schumann substantially enriched the music of his last years—for instance, the *Manfred* and *Faust* overtures—by the injection of Bachian phraseology. Even late Chopin was touched by Bach and few German composers since then have escaped his influence, which soon became a natural one. But Mahler's consciousness of tradition and the deliberate historicism of Max Reger were surely in the long run unfortunate for them, and the historical sense seems to have weighed upon Schoenberg so heavily that he had to make a violent effort to throw off its tyranny.

* * *

All this is not the working of tradition as I have been considering it: the slow, natural, almost imperceptible process by which the art of Western music has been transmitted from generation to generation and modified here and there by national characteristics and the rubbing off of one national characteristic on to another, a process which emerges into clear consciousness usually only when someone revolts against it. Our tradition has been accumulated not by deliberate efforts of anyone's will but rather as a coral reef is built up, except that the course of musical tradition is marked by some very outsize polyps. We usually think of music not as streams of evolution but as the sum of the work of individual composers, and although, to quote Eliot again (and for the last time), 'the current does not at all flow invariably through the most distinguished reputations', I want to consider how two or three of the 'most distinguished reputations' stand in relation to the current. All the great masters have derived from the tradition. Some have affected it much more than others: for instance, Beethoven very much more than Mozart. This has nothing to do with relative 'greatness', which is not a measurable quality anyhow. Beethoven possessed qualities that specially appealed to the romantic age, which was an age of strife and heroics; the heritage of Mozart failed to thrive in the climate of the French Revolutionary and Napoleonic wars and was taken up by minor escapist talents like Hummel. But all the great masters did something to the tradition, gave it a new twist or brought some phase of it to a perfection which exists in itself to delight but which exhausted its capacity for development, so that it dwindled in the hands of epigones. (As indeed might have happened with Mozart, without any help from the French Revolution.) The works of the masters are the crises of tradition.

I must make it clear that I am not thinking merely of style. Style is only the phenomenon, but in music we are constantly obliged to talk about it because of the extreme elusiveness of the noumenon. Because the vital essence of music defies formulation in words, we analyse and describe the styles in which it manifests itself and are apt to confuse the one with the other. They are not identical but they are inseparable. So in relating individual composers with tradition, I am obliged to speak mostly in terms of style although my real concern is with the intangibles, imponderables and indefinables that have gone to form it. Perhaps I can best make my meaning clear if I go back to an example I have already used, and suggest that Schumann's piano fugues merely ape Bach's style while the *Manfred* overture and the *adagio* of the *Rhenish* Symphony carry on something of Bach's ethos as well as his phraseology. Instances of the taking over of a master's style without an inkling of his ethos are numerous and obvious; it has happened with Palestrina, with Handel, with Wagner, perhaps with most outstanding composers. It is not too difficult to write fake Palestrina, but only a creative talent of an extremely high order could capture the ethos of *Assumpta est Maria* and the other great Masses. There are probably many instances of the reverse, though by their nature they are far less obvious and are hardly ever demonstrable. I will, however, suggest that Dvořák's relationship to Schubert is such a case of the ethos without the style.

One of the most familiar instances of a master whose work constitutes a major crisis of tradition is, of course, Beethoven. It is not difficult to see how he stood as a young man in relation to the great German instrumental tradition, for he was first, last and, in spite of *Fidelio* and the *Missa solemnis*, nearly all the time an instrumental composer. His conception of musical structure and texture, the nature of his themes and so on derive from Haydn (much more than from Mozart), from C. P. E. Bach, from his teacher Neefe and Aloys Förster, and at least one non-German, Cherubini, as well as from a crowd of lesser men with whom he must have been familiar though we forget them. He also inherited from them an ethos which one very inadequately indicates by such words as '*Sturm und Drang*', 'tragic passion', 'controlled fire', 'heroic serenity', 'moral fervour'. He came into this tradition of style and ethos, and even if he had never come into it, it would have continued. It is difficult to think of early nineteenth-century music without Beethoven, but it is not impossible. (It is quite easy to think of the late eighteenth century without Bach; to all intents and purposes it *was* without Bach.) We must be circumspect about composers who may have been influenced by Beethoven, such men as Prince Louis Ferdinand of Prussia and Jan Václav Voříšek, though none of them was influenced by that which was unique in him. But we are still left with such music as

Cherubini's *Médée* and the wonderful E flat melodrama in *Les deux journées*:

Ex. 26

Sostenuto assai

the first movement of Clementi's B minor Sonata and the slow movement of Dussek's in F minor, Op. 77, to show how much we commonly think of as Beethovenish really belongs to the spirit of his age. The tradition would have continued if Beethoven had never existed—but how differently. Other composers would have hit on Beethoven's supposed innovations in the symphony. They would have harked back to the scherzo in the finale; Haydn had already done it in his no. 46 in B major. They would have introduced the chorus; Peter von Winter had already done so in his *Battle Symphony* of 1814. But the Haydn and the Winter are only unimportant incidents in the history of the symphony; Beethoven's Fifth and Ninth were crises after which the symphony could never be the same again. (Symphonies like Donizetti's and Gounod's and Bizet's only show how far the Latins stood outside the main, now essentially Germanic, instrumental tradition.) The impact of these things was not immediately apparent, nor was that of the last piano sonatas, still less that of the last string quartets. At first it was superficial.

Mendelssohn cast his *Hymn of Praise* in the form of a symphony with choral finale; Berlioz opened the finale of *Harold in Italy* with reminiscences of the three earlier movements. Before long the impact was much deeper and almost all-pervading. It was far more than a matter of novel forms and textures or an unprecedented motivic development of *durchbrochene Arbeit*. The symphony was no longer simply a four-movement composition for orchestra; it was a heroic or pastoral poem, an autobiographical document, a vision of all-human brotherhood. The soloist in the piano concerto was no longer simply a pianist; he was an heroic figure who pleaded with the orchestra or challenged it or led it in triumph. The last piano sonatas extended fugue and variation into areas where they had never ventured before and the last quartets carried musical thought into a sphere the very existence of which had never been suspected. Even a composer like Schumann, whose natural gifts were utterly different from Beethoven's, felt impelled to go against his own grain; it was not enough for him to take a handful of what might have been Beethoven piano-music, like 'Grillen' in the *Fantasie-stücke*, and play with it whimsically; he must needs take the aphorisms that came naturally to him and try to develop them dialectically in long movements. Brahms, who approached nearer to Beethoven's ethos than most of the successors, often sidestepped the problem of musical dialectics and instead of 'development' employed variation —'continuous variation' as Schoenberg called it—on a scale and in a manner unknown before, which was perhaps *his* most important and enduring enrichment of tradition. Wagner seized on one element, that striving to make instrumental music more precisely expressive which had begun with C. P. E. Bach, concluded that Beethoven had confessed failure by turning to words in the finale of the Ninth, and devised an art in long stretches of which a stream of quasi-symphonic music is made explicit not only by words but by stage-action. Few composers have owed more to tradition and at the same time imposed themselves on it and enlarged it more masterfully than Beethoven.

Not even Wagner. Wagner stood more squarely in the centre of the main stream than Beethoven, for Beethoven was overwhelmingly Germanic in his origins. But Wagner, very German as he was,

was more susceptible to the influence of that 'welscher Dunst' and 'welscher Tand' which Hans Sachs warns against at the end of *Die Meistersinger*. Sachs was foolish, for that dilution of the purely German tradition by Italian cantilena was quite normal and often beneficial. Not many Germans have been as deeply Italianized as Handel and Mozart, but few of them from Schütz to Henze have escaped it. Wagner enjoyed a long love-hatred for Bellini and absorbed a great deal of Italianism at second-hand through Weber. And his eclecticism spread roots much wider than these: to Auber and Halévy, to the Parisian grand opera of Spontini and Meyerbeer which was itself a monster of eclecticism, though the central trunk of Wagner's music was solidly German. I have already suggested that 'the ability to absorb without becoming saturated is one of the surest indices of a country's musical well-being' and it is by no means a sign of weakness in an individual composer. It is this mingling of national streams which enables us to go on speaking of a 'European' or 'Western' tradition; the tradition was not merely Western in origin, it continued to be 'Western'. Perhaps because of this eclecticism, Wagner's positive and perceptible influence on the tradition, though not as deep and enduring as Beethoven's, was more widespread. Beethoven was admired and performed from London and Paris to St. Petersburg, and quite early in the United States, but it was only in the German lands that composers seriously tried to walk in his footsteps.

Wagner was different. His ethos, made verbally explicit if not lucid in his prose-writings, ran like quicksilver through European culture and stirred violent passions of adoration and dissent. His techniques were seized upon by musicians of every country whether or not they had any true conception, or any conception at all, of his ethos. The French Wagnerians—the Chabrier of *Gwendoline*, Chausson, d'Indy—came nearest among non-Germans to understanding it, but in every country where opera was written composers tried to eliminate the set-number and the contrast of song with recitative, to make the orchestra more important and to give it themes to play in association with the characters of the drama. They employed more adventurous harmony and studied Wagner's methods of scoring. They imagined they were being 'Wagnerian' and the public was quite sure they were; in fact the mere doing of any of these things was in itself enough to attract accusations of Wagnerism against such men as Bizet and the mature Verdi who were quite innocent of the charge.

The paradox is that hardly any of these things was peculiarly Wagnerian. They belonged to the period generally. They had begun before Wagner and they would no doubt have continued and developed if he had never existed. The tendencies to fuse the set-numbers of opera and to melt down recitative and aria had already been strong not only in German romantic opera but in French grand opera and even Italian opera. At a time when Wagner was still a musically illiterate schoolboy, both Spohr and Weber had written through-composed operas, *Der Berggeist* and *Euryanthe*, in which the orchestral parts were of great importance. Musical ideas associated with characters have been known in opera from very early days, actually as early as Lully's *Persée* of 1682 which has a figure that heralds Medusa's appearance in Act III, is heard before Mercury's air when he puts her to sleep, and appears again when her sister-Gorgons come to avenge her:

Ex. 27 *(a)*

(c)

The device was very common in French and German opera in the early nineteenth century and the idea was well understood by such critics as E. T. A. Hoffmann and Castil-Blaze. Transformation of such motives was also well known; Weber practised it in *Euryanthe* and Schubert in *Fierrabras*. Chromatic harmony, appoggiatura harmony, extension of tonality by foreign chords and progressions, were all employed by Chopin and Liszt and the later Schumann. Wagner's rich orchestral quasi-polyphony was new, but strong 'horizontal' tendencies had already begun to make themselves felt through 'vertical' harmony, for instance in late Chopin. And the valve-horn (which is the main ingredient in the warm, full sound of Wagner's inside parts) existed for anyone to experiment with. There can be no doubt that lesser men would have continued working along all these lines if there had never been a Wagner, and no doubt that they would sometimes have combined them. Wagner actually combined them. And because he did so in works of outstanding genius he produced a crisis in tradition, in fact a whole series of crises: in opera as an art-form, in the orchestra as a medium, in the very language of music. Like Beethoven he distilled the spirit of his age.

* * *

This is the natural relationship of the genius to tradition. His work is born out of it, transcends it, and gives it a new dynamism and sometimes a new direction. To go back to my parable of the folk-singer and the folk-song, the genius is like a singer who gives a marvellous new twist, a new turn of phrase to the tune, which makes his version of it the most remembered. But it is not great creative ability alone that makes a composer specially potent in his impact on tradition; there are also the factors of time and environment which can work negatively as well as positively. Both Palestrina and Handel contributed incalculably to the ethos of Western music but neither can be said to have had a dynamic effect on tradition. Each brought a style to perfection at the wrong point in history, when it had already begun to exhaust itself and to be superseded by new and more vigorous styles. The crisis in their works is the crisis of the wave at its highest point before it curls over and collapses. Handel's dynamic transformation of oratorio was made to the wrong form at the wrong time and in the wrong place. His oratorios were so cleverly tailored for the Protestant middle-class British audience that they have never made a wide and lasting impression outside the English-speaking world. (I have never forgotten being told by a music-loving German lady in Cologne in the 1920s that she had recently heard a beautiful unknown work by Handel; it turned out to be *Messiah*.) If Handel had written Italian oratorios and English operas, he might have saved English music from provincialism and many of his own greatest works from near-oblivion. Bach also brought a style to perfection at the wrong moment in history and perhaps it was his good fortune to be almost forgotten by the next generation; the impact of his later discovery was so much the greater.

It may happen that a smaller talent in a more limited environment can, especially if he comes at the right time, contribute more obviously to tradition—I say 'more obviously', not 'more'—than a genius who has come at the wrong time. Glinka is a case in point. He was the purest product of that Russian tradition I have described, the tradition compounded of foreign opera with native folk-music and practised by foreign professionals and native dilettanti. His mental furniture was not at all unlike Wagner's: the classical German symphonies and the operas of Weber, Bellini, and Donizetti. By the originality of his talent he made a dynamic impact on the Russian tradition which, within its much narrower limits, was not so very much less than Wagner's on European music in general. Even its perceptible influence has been equally long-lasting, as Stravinsky has testified. But it was limited to a peripheral tradition which in

Glinka's day, as in our own, flowed somewhat apart from the main stream.

Another Russian composer will serve to illustrate the point that the seemingly most original genius also owes a considerable debt to tradition. When a composer appears to have no ancestors, it is usually because we happen to be ignorant of the ancestors. When Debussy, in a famous phrase, likened Mussorgsky to a savage discovering music at each step taken by his imagination, he was making precisely the same mistake—and, as it happens, in a very similar phrase—as Wagner when he said that Berlioz was 'obliged to feel his way in a fantastic labyrinth'. What Mussorgsky did lack was the technical training which provides a musician with the routine facility that can be the bad side of tradition; lacking it, he had to sweat much harder to construct an extended work or even to make neat joins in a short one. On the other hand, his want of technical facility may have forced him into intense self-reliance, just as Beethoven was ultimately forced by his deafness. But Mussorgsky was no savage discovering music through his fingers at the piano, although he did discover a lot of unorthodox, expressive harmony in that way. He knew the major European classics—and romantics. He knew Glinka and Dargomïzhsky, and he knew Meyerbeerian grand opera both at first hand and through Serov, the most Meyerbeerian of his Russian contemporaries. He once wrote a very scathing letter about Serov's *Judith*, because the older men of his circle, of whom he stood in awe, detested *Judith*[7]; but the letter hardly expresses his sincere reaction, for his earliest serious attempt at opera, *Salammbô*, was written under the direct influence of *Judith*—and a good deal of the music of *Salammbô* was afterwards transferred to *Boris Godunov*. As for the genre, as distinct from the music, of *Boris* and *Khovanshchina*, it can only be distraction by the novelties of idiom and treatment that prevents our seeing them as 'grand operas', just as without too much difficulty we can see *Götterdämmerung* to be. It is pleasant to reflect that neither *Götterdämmerung* nor *Boris* nor *Aïda* would have been quite what it is without Meyerbeer. But magpie composers like Meyerbeer often play a part in the transmission of tradition that

---

[7] See *Essays presented to Egon Wellesz* (ed. J. A. Westrup) (Oxford, 1966), p. 171.

is in the long run much more important than their contribution to the ethos. It is possible that history may pass this verdict on Stravinsky, who has been in some respects the Meyerbeer of our day.

Composers of this type are foci in the literal sense of the word: points on which rays of tradition converge and from which they proceed. When they bring to a focus what we may call fashionable tendencies, they naturally enjoy immediate popularity. Meyerbeer, who consciously concerned himself only with the styles of the day and a little before, was affected—if only slightly—by the beginnings of historicism at the time. He symbolized the Calvinists in *Les Huguenots* by a Lutheran chorale—and the unpedantic Parisian public recognized 'Ein' feste Burg' as Protestant though they might not have recognized a Calvinist psalm-tune; he symbolized the Anabaptists in *Le Prophète* by a sort of chorale of his own. These are only clumsy stumblings towards a sense of music's past, but they should be compared with the tune that is Blondel's theme-song in Grétry's *Richard Coeur-de-Lion*; Grétry had not the faintest notion what a twelfth-century *trouvère* song was like, and I don't suppose he had the faintest care.

Stravinsky, being a man of the twentieth century, had a very lively sense of the past. He began by focusing the strongest contemporary rays of Russian music: Rimsky-Korsakov and Skryabin. As he went on to become a cosmopolitan, he absorbed everything truly contemporary, including ragtime, except the unfashionably German; he also showed a growing awareness of the Russian past, including Glinka (as in *Mavra*), and then of the European past, beginning with Pergolesi (or pseudo-Pergolesi). Later still, always in step with contemporary interests, his sensitive antennae picked up not only Webern but Gesualdo and Machaut. A composer with such a gift for absorbing from six centuries of our music elements that were congenial both to himself and to his public, and by force of re-creative effort making them his own, has come as close as any musician I can think of to Eliot's ideal of continual surrender to something more valuable, of continual extinction of personality.

It is a wry comment on the present state of the German tradition that it figures so microscopically in the Stravinskian synthesis, not because of Stravinsky's imperfect sympathy with the Teutonic but because his synthesis so faithfully reflects contemporary views. The last great representative of the nearly pure German tradition was Brahms. (The weaknesses of Bruckner derive from his heritage of a narrower, really provincial tradition, that of Austrian church music, which shows in his slow harmonic pace and his block orchestration.) Brahms inherited nearly all his qualities from the great German past but, in striking contrast to Wagner, very little from anything else. (Brahms and Wagner stand in much the same relation to each other as Palestrina and Lassus.) He is a classic case of a master, a real master, too conscious of responsibility towards tradition in a rather limited sense and of his self-imposed duty to preserve its values at a time when they were being challenged by the so-called 'New German School' of Liszt and his followers. He fulfilled his duty so well that he will always command the affection of those who are specially attached to the German tradition, but he has paid the usual penalty of the conservative in that he was unable to contribute much to its continuance technically, beyond that combination of variation with development which fascinated Schoenberg. If you merely conserve, you don't perpetuate. Like Palestrina and Handel, Brahms was a terminus rather than a junction.

The generation after Brahms—Strauss, Mahler, Reger, Schoenberg—sought in their various ways, by injection of foreign elements or very new ones or very old ones, to revitalize the German tradition, but the only lasting result of their efforts has been something that has no roots in anything specifically German: the twelve-note idea. Whether or not he originated it, Schoenberg grasped it in a convulsive effort to make a decisive break with that suffocating sense of tradition which threatened to overwhelm him as it had overwhelmed Brahms. We must not be misled by the facts that twelve-note music was a product of German culture; that Schoenberg himself thought he had discovered a means of 'assuring the pre-eminence of German music for a hundred years'[8]; and that the German in him very soon absorbed and digested the foreign body,

[8] H. H. Stuckenschmidt, *Arnold Schönberg* (Zürich, 1951), p. 64.

as it did in Alban Berg's case too. The twelve-note idea has since amply proved its seminal value in non-German contexts. And the twelve-note idea, with the general serialism that has developed from it, is of outstanding importance to us because its appearance possibly initiated the beginning of the end of the Western tradition of music.

*   *   *

That may sound like the enunciation of an excessively narrow, conservative, and pessimistic judgement. It is not intended to be. I must explain why I think it is an objective statement of a position that we have to face. I have just used the term 'foreign body'. Serialism was the first of a number of new concepts—electronic music, aleatoric music, stochastic music, computerized music—which are in themselves totally foreign to the Western tradition: usually foreign in techniques, always foreign in ethos. The questions are: To what extent will the Western tradition be able to absorb these foreign bodies? And if it rejects them, will they develop separate existences and ultimately supplant it? The history of serial music shows the process by which a foreign body can be absorbed. The earliest twelve-note music, Schoenberg's *Klavierstücke*, Op. 23, was at first totally meaningless to the listener because the succession of notes and the coincidence of notes were deliberately dissociated from all previous melodic lines and harmonies; any resemblance to living music was purely coincidental. With one exception: rhythm. Schoenberg would write, say, a waltz that was indeed in triple time and waltz-tempo and with waltz-like rhythmic patterns. Where there was not even a rhythmic clue, the music was as meaningless as some abstruse Asian music to the Western listener. Then several things happened. Schoenberg, and still more successfully Alban Berg, found means of making the physical sound of twelve-note music less desiccated. Then, when ears had learned to tolerate the physical sound and became accustomed to the idiom, they began to perceive meanings in the new relationship of the notes to each other. Twelve-note music was beginning to establish an ethos of its own, even, as in Berg's Violin Concerto, a means of communicating a message. The usual pattern of popularization followed: through the enthusiasm and propaganda of what I have called the dynamic nucleus, a wider public has learned at least to tolerate Schoenberg even if it doesn't leave the opera-house humming tunes from *Moses und Aron*. As regards the serial idiom in general, they were probably helped to accept it by the practice of more conservative composers who inserted twelve-note elements in non-serial works, as Samuel Barber did in his Piano Sonata.

The same pattern may be followed with electronic music, aleatoric music, and computerized music in so far as they have points of significant identity with traditional music. Even though such identities may be misleading, there exists a possibility of communication between composer and audience and a possibility of extending the audience. When electronic sounds are used as an adjunct to traditional music, there is no difficulty at all; they are nothing more than a sophistication of the old theatrical wind-machine which Marschner introduced in *Hans Heiling* and Wagner in *The Flying Dutchman* and Strauss translated from the opera-house to the concert-hall in *Don Quixote*. But pure electronic music has no points of identity with music as we have known it. As I have already suggested, the electronic composer is starting from scratch, like Stone Age man. He is experimenting with sounds for his own personal satisfaction. He may share his pleasure with colleagues who are playing with sound in the same way and he may arouse wonder and interest among the bystanders, but he cannot communicate with them yet. He is heavily handicapped by the fact that, while he may be able to wash his own mind and ears clean of the traditional associations of music, he has to live in a world of listeners who have not been mind-washed and ear-washed. It is significant that, at any rate in London, the small, highly enthusiastic audiences who attend concerts of such music consist almost entirely of young people of a type one hardly ever sees at more conventional concerts, youngsters who are excited by the pure phenomena of unprecedented sounds.

This is vitally important, for it suggests that in such audiences of the musically naïve young, many of whom are possibly quite uninterested in traditional music or know it only in the form of 'pop', the extreme *avant-garde* composer may find the dynamic nucleus which will activate the wider audience of the future. Even if his kind of art remains totally dissociated from everything in music as we know it, there is no reason why it should not develop its own techniques, build up in the course of time its own associations, and so create its own ethos. I have spoken rather frivolously of the beginnings of a totally new music, but they are symptoms of a crisis which all of us who are concerned with music must study with the utmost seriousness.

Is our great tradition of Western music really coming to an end? Is it even now mainly living on its past? The frantic search for new techniques and styles is itself a symptom of malaise. In the distant past it took a long time to exhaust a style. The pace has been gradually speeding up and since the Second World War it has become bewildering. We cannot afford to be complacent about the present situation in which great sums of money have to be spent to keep alive institutions like opera-houses and symphony orchestras originally brought into existence by a very different society from the one we live in and by media in which our most advanced composers are not much interested. In other words, opera-houses and symphony orchestras are imperceptibly slipping into the position of museums for the safeguarding of the great music of the past. To my mind, and no doubt to yours, this is obviously very necessary; and the great public would be bewildered by the suggestion that orchestras and opera-houses could become obsolescent, for the great mass of the public still wants just this—the music of the past. But the necessity may not be so obvious to the young generation, the generation which attaches less value to tradition than any generation we know of. As we are all very conscious—not only in America, not only in Britain, but all over the world where they have an opportunity to speak out— we are confronted with a generation that wants a clean break with tradition of every kind: in the values of capitalism and communism, in moral values, and in the values of art and learning. The nature of a university is

to be of the past, to teach the past and to get the students to agree to study and evaluate the past, to take the past seriously as an immense fund of richness which we cannot, in the nature of the case, have today. But the modern student will not do this. He does not want any more of the past. He wants the future. For the modern student, the university is quite simply there to study, and even to create, the future. But that is just what a university cannot do. That runs against its entire idea, which is essentially concerned with tradition. The new university of the students would be without tradition. It would be a pure study of potentiality.[9]

In such a university the ideal professor would be the Merlin of T. H. White's amusing novel *The Sword in the Stone*, the magician who could foresee the future but had a frightful memory for the past.

I am no Merlin myself. The normal apparatus of scholarship does not include a crystal ball. But it is safe to say that such a climate of intellectual opinion, which is the climate we shall move into unless this generation changes its mind drastically as it grows older, would be very favourable for the development of purely electronic music, computerized music, and all the other manifestations which some of us view with apprehension. It is a climate in which the tradition of Western music could hardly survive very long and its masterpieces would ultimately be preserved not in old-fashioned concert-halls and opera-houses but on sound tapes. It seems a bleak prospect. And yet, as the cultures of mankind assimilate more and more, the non-Western traditions of music may wither too, as those of architecture are doing already, and give an opportunity for some new music, electronic or not, beginning with totally new associations, to lay the foundations of a *world* tradition. Whether such a tradition could develop as a genuinely universal music or would remain the possession of an intellectual class while the rest of humanity would console itself with the decadent relics of the old music—that would depend on humanity itself and the course it decides to take.

[9] Roger Poole, 'Universities and the Future', *Manchester Guardian Weekly*, 6 February 1969.

INDEX

Index

Schütz, Heinrich, 18, 36, 39, 70, 97, 116
Schweitzer, Albert, 7
Serov, A. N., 120
Sgambati, Giovanni, 66
Shakespeare, William, 83, 94, 106
Sharp, Cecil, 2, 4
Shaw, Bernard, 17–18
Shostakovich, D. D., 55
Sigismund III (of Poland), 36
Skryabin, A. N., 19, 77, 121
Smetana, Bedřich, 67, 71–2, 75
Smolensky, S. V., 47n
Spinaccino, Francesco, 90
Spohr, Louis, 117
Spontini, Gaspare, 98, 116
Stäblein, Bruno, 9n
Stockhausen, Karlheinz, 60
Stradella, Alessandro, 66
Strauss, Richard, 18, 111, 122, 124
Stravinsky, Igor, 3, 111, 119, 121–2
Strunk, Oliver, 8on
Stuckenschmidt, H. H., 122n
Sullivan, Sir Arthur, 101
Sumarokov, A. P., 49–50
Susato, Tylman, 89
Svyatoslav II (of Kiev), 45
Sweelinck, J. P., 19, 35, 38
Sychra, Antonín, 73n

Tchaïkovsky, see Chaykovsky
Thibaut, Justus, 107
Titov, N. A., 52
Titov, Vasily, 47
Tolstoy, Count L. N., 58–9
Tomašek, V. J., 72
Trutovsky, V. F., 49–50
Tutankhamun, 85

Ulïbïshev, A. D., 52, 56

Vecchi, Giuseppe, 27
Verdelot, Philippe, 36
Verdi, Giuseppe, 17–18, 62, 66, 100, 101, 116
Verstovsky, A. N., 54
Victoria, T. L. de, 36
Villa-Lobos, Heitor, 20
Virgil, 83
Vitry, Philippe de, 45
Vivaldi, Antonio, 38, 97
Volkonsky, Andrey, 60
Voříšek, J. V., 72, 113

Wagner, Peter, 8n
Wagner, Richard, 18, 40, 66, 70, 76, 78, 98–9, 101, 108–110, 113, 115–120, 122, 124
Weber, C. M. von, 40, 76, 116–9
Webern, Anton von, 121
Weisse, Michael, 8
Wellesz, Egon, 12on
Westrup, Sir Jack, 12on
White, T. H., 126
Wielhorski, Counts Mateusz and Michal, 52
Willaert, Adrian, 36
Winter, Peter von, 114
Wolf, Hugo, 92
Wolkenstein, Oswald von, 32
Wolzogen, Hans von, 99n

Yatsuhashi, 42

Zarlino, Gioseffe, 47